Passenger Aircraft and Airlines

by John Taylor
and Susan Young

Marshall Cavendish London & New York

Published by Marshall Cavendish Publications
Limited,
58, Old Compton Street,
London W1V 5PA

© Marshall Cavendish Publications Limited 1975

First printing 1975

ISBN 0 85685 142 6

Printed in Great Britain by
Ben Johnson & Company Limited

Picture Research : Linda Proud

We gratefully acknowledge all airline
companies who have contributed
photographs for this book, also the
following sources :

1	Air France
2/3	Port Authority of NY & NJ
4	Colorific /John Moss
8/9	Novosti
11-13	John Taylor
16/17	Flight International
18/19	Air France
20/21	John Taylor
22	Central Office Information
24/25	John Taylor
32(c)	John Taylor
26	Novosti
37(t)	Novosti
37(b)	John Taylor
38/39(t)	Flight International
41	Flight International
42-43	Hawker Siddeley Aviation Ltd.
44	John Taylor
51(t)	John Taylor
56/57	John Taylor
70/71	McDonnel Douglas Corporation
78/79	John Taylor
92/93	John Taylor
97	Boeing
102	Boeing
106	Finnair
109-110	Boeing
116	Laker
121	John Taylor
122	Hawker Siddeley Aviation Ltd.
132	Hawker Siddeley Aviation Ltd.

The Boeing 747 is the largest airliner in service and can
carry up to five hundred passengers. It is powered by four
Pratt and Whitney JT9D turbofan engines, which use a front
mounted fan to blow air around the main engine, so that it
mixes with the hot exhaust, improving both quietness and
fuel economy.

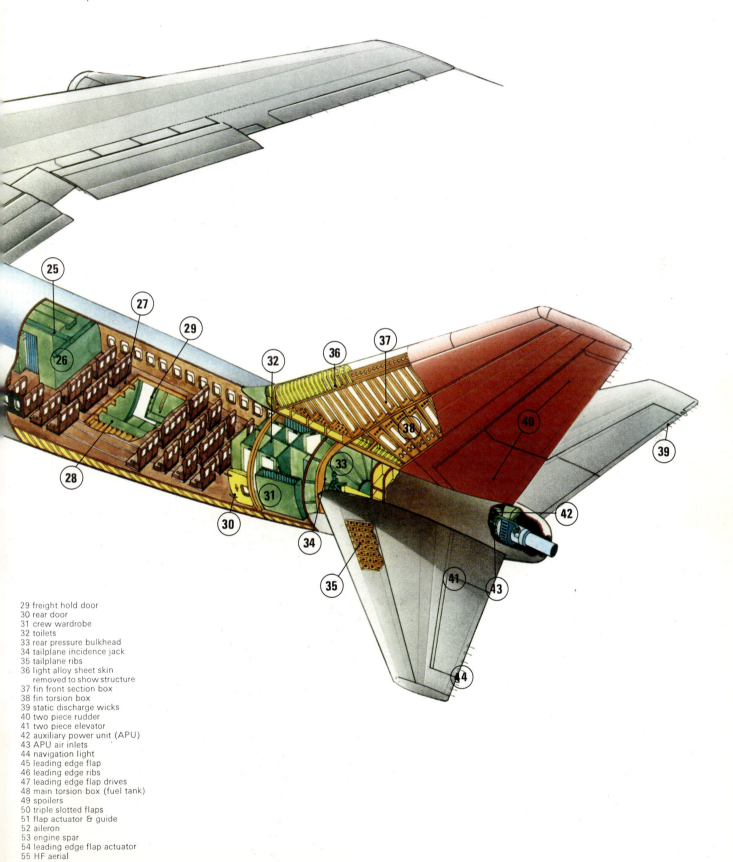

29 freight hold door
30 rear door
31 crew wardrobe
32 toilets
33 rear pressure bulkhead
34 tailplane incidence jack
35 tailplane ribs
36 light alloy sheet skin
   removed to show structure
37 fin front section box
38 fin torsion box
39 static discharge wicks
40 two piece rudder
41 two piece elevator
42 auxiliary power unit (APU)
43 APU air inlets
44 navigation light
45 leading edge flap
46 leading edge ribs
47 leading edge flap drives
48 main torsion box (fuel tank)
49 spoilers
50 triple slotted flaps
51 flap actuator & guide
52 aileron
53 engine spar
54 leading edge flap actuator
55 HF aerial

Contents

Previous Pages *Night time at Orly Airport, Paris, for a line of Air France Caravelles, used on that airline's short range services.*

Above *John F Kennedy (previously Idlewild) Airport, New York, on a typically busy day.*

Overleaf *The view from the cockpit of one of British Caledonian's fleet of BAC1-11s, 'Royal Burgh of Dunfermline'.*

Introduction

Commercial aircraft have become more than a mere means of transporting people. They are symbols of all that is excellent in modern electronics and engineering; they are a constant reminder of man's power to progress; they are advertisements for their airlines and the excitement of international travel; and they are airborne representatives of the complexities of twentieth-century society.

The days have long gone when, paraphrasing Henry Ford, you could have an airliner any colour, as long as it was raw aluminium. Today the visitor to an international airport is dazzled by the variety of colour schemes and the high standard of their design. Impact and ingenuity are two of the most important factors, although some motifs are more impressive than others. Iran Air features an ancient symbol, the Homa Bird, Nigeria a delightful 'flying elephant' and Qantas, predictably, a 'flying kangaroo'. Among other intriguing designs are the stark but beautiful raw metallic of American Airlines, the subtly-toned blues of KLM, and Canadian Pacific's unique diagonals.

In the rapidly changing world of aviation it is never possible to say that a list of aircraft or airlines is totally comprehensive, or thoroughly up-to-date. In any month some major operator will change its colour scheme, a once world-renowned aircraft will fly for the last time, or a sudden merger will spell the end of a familiar name and, perhaps, the emergence of another.

In the passenger aircraft section of this book, over three dozen of the world's most common long-distance scheduled airliners have been carefully detailed and illustrated. None of the jets in daily service with major operators has escaped attention, and the more common survivors from the piston and turboprop generation are also here. Inevitably, some planes that may occasionally still be seen in operation are missing, and some, like the Convair 990A, may not be in service with any scheduled operator beyond 1975.

The Comet will almost certainly have disappeared from passenger routes by 1976 signifying the end of a link with the world's first jet passenger aircraft. The Convair 440, 580 and 640 series, along with the Douglas DC-4, DC-6 and DC-7 and the Lockheed L-1049 Super Constellation occasionally emerge from freight services to be seen on domestic passenger flights in various parts of the world, while even a plane introduced as recently as the Vanguard has already been virtually relegated solely to freight service.

As a guide, the airline section has been designed to cover all the jets likely to be seen on scheduled passenger services at the world's major airports in 1975 and all of the propeller and turboprop craft likely to be still working scheduled services at the end of the decade.

The airline section comprises over 100 carefully-selected operators, including all the major international airlines, the larger independent and non-scheduled firms (charter subsidiaries of scheduled airlines are usually mentioned along with their parent), and any strictly domestic airline whose sheer size justifies inclusion. At least nine out of every ten planes to be seen today at any major airport will certainly belong to one of the airlines featured here.

This book does not, therefore, pretend to be a planespotter's bible. That would be impossible. Instead, it is a spectacularly colourful, informative and readable guide to commercial aviation, the planes that transport the world's travellers, and the organizations that operate them. It is the perfect companion for a visit that anyone, anywhere in the world, could take to his or her local airport.

The world's major commercial aircraft

Airbus (A300B)

Large-capacity short/medium-range airliner, operated by Air France, Air Siam, Iberia, Lufthansa, SATA of Switzerland, Sterling Airways of Denmark, Transbrasil and Trans European Airways of Belgium. This European Airbus which entered commercial service in 1973 is built by companies in five countries, with engines from a sixth. Aerospatiale of France, MBB and VFW-Fokker of Germany, Fokker-VFW of the Netherlands and CASA of Spain received loans from their governments to finance design and manufacture. Hawker Siddeley Aviation of the UK, responsible for the wings, has had to finance its work privately. The turbofan engines come from the USA, as the original plan to fit Rolls-Royce RB.211s was abandoned when the UK government decided not to participate in the project.

Engines: Two General Electric CF6-50C turbofans, each giving 51,000 pounds (23,130kg) of thrust, in underwing pods.
Maximum cruising speed: 582mph (937km/h) at a height of 25,000ft (7,620m).
Typical range: 1,615 miles (2,600km) with 281 passengers.
Accommodation: Flight crew of two or three. Up to 345 passengers.
Orders: Firm orders for 21 aircraft (11 A300B2 as described, 10 longer-range A300B4). Options on 17 more B2s and 8 B4s in 1975.

Below The first Airbus to enter commercial service was F-BVGA for Air France, which also incorporated that airline's revised colour scheme. The Airbus is the only one of the four 'wide-bodied' jets in production that relies on two engines as opposed to the three of the DC-10 and TriStar and four of the 747.

Antonov An-24

Short-range airliner, used widely on local services in eastern Europe, the Soviet Union and Cuba. A few operate in Africa, the Middle East and China. This neat twin-turboprop transport was designed in the late 1950s to replace piston-engined types like the Il-12, Il-14 and Li-2 (Russian-built DC-3) on Aeroflot's internal routes. It entered service in September 1963, since when several hundred have been delivered for commercial and military use. Aeroflot's An-24Vs alone had carried more than 50 million passengers and half a million tons of freight by 1971. The An-24T is a freighter, with underbelly loading door and folding seats along the cabin walls.
Engines: Two 2,550hp Ivchenko AI-24A turboprops. An-24RV and An-24RT versions also have an RU 19-300 auxiliary turbojet in the rear of the starboard nacelle, mainly to improve take-off from hot or high airfields.
Maximum cruising speed: 280mph (450km/h) at a height of 19,700ft (6,000m).
Typical range: 341 miles (550km) with 50 passengers.
Accommodation: Flight crew of two to five, and 44–50 passengers.
Orders: Aeroflot is believed to have about 400 An-24s. Export sales total about 75 for 14 airlines in 13 countries.

BAC 1-11

Short/medium-range airliner, operated on scheduled services and on holiday charter flights by airlines in Europe and throughout the world. BAC intended the One-Eleven to be the jet successor to the Viscount. It encountered far more competition than that pioneer turboprop airliner, but got off to a good start in the early 1960s with initial orders from British United Airways and the US airlines Braniff and Mohawk. It first entered commercial service in 1965. The original Series 200 has Spey 506 engines and carries up to 89 passengers. The Series 300, and the 400 for American operators, have uprated Spey 511s. The 500 has a 5ft (1.52m) greater wing span, longer fuselage and further-uprated Spey 512DWs. The Series 475 combines the original fuselage with the 500's wing and engines.

Engines (Series 500): Two Rolls-Royce Spey 512DW turbofans, each giving 12,550 pounds (5,692kg) of thrust, in pods on sides of rear fuselage.

Maximum cruising speed (all versions): 541mph (871km/h) at a height of 21,000 ft. (6,400m).

Typical range (Series 500): 1,705 miles (2,744km) with full payload.

Accommodation (Series 500): Flight crew of two and up to 119 passengers.

Orders: Total of 217 sold by 1975.

Boeing 707

Long-range airliner, operated throughout the world by most of the major international airlines. The Boeing 707 was the third jet airliner to enter service, (in 1958) after Britain's Comet and the Soviet Tu-104. Initial version was the 707-120, powered by 13,500 pound (6,124kg) thrust JT3C-6 turbojets, seating up to 181 passengers, and intended for use on US internal routes. Next came the 707-220 with more powerful JT4A engines, and the longer, intercontinental 707-320 and 420 with JT4A and Rolls-Royce Conway engines respectively. A switch to turbofan engines produced the 707-120B, 707-320B and 707-320C passenger/freighter, which continues in production.

Engines (707-320C): Four Pratt & Whitney JT3D-3B turbofans, each giving 18,000 pounds (8,165kg) of thrust, in underwing pods.

Maximum cruising speed (707-320C): 600 mph (965km/h) at a height of 25,000ft (7,620m).

Typical range (707-320C): 3,925 miles (6,320km) with a full payload.

Accommodation (707-320C): Flight crew of three to five. Up to 202 passengers or 13 pallets of freight.

Orders: Total of 739 sold by the beginning of 1975.

Boeing 720

Medium-range airliner, operated throughout the world. Although barely distinguishable from the 707-120 in size and appearance, the Boeing 720 was redesigned for use on shorter routes and entered service in 1960. Needing less fuel load, it could be built with a much lighter structure; and an improved wing gave it a higher cruising speed and better take-off performance. Sixty-five basic 720s were produced first, with JT3C turbojets. Subsequent aircraft were delivered as 720Bs, with JT3D turbofans, and ten of the 720s were re-engined. Main operators were American airlines such as United, Eastern, American, Western and Northwest Orient; but other sales and resales have taken 720s as far afield as Ethiopia, Israel and Pakistan.

Engines (720B): Four Pratt & Whitney JT3D-3 turbofans, each giving 18,000 pounds (8,165kg) of thrust, in underwing pods.

Maximum cruising speed (720B): 611mph (983km/h) at a height of 25,000ft (7,620m).

Typical range (720B): 4,155 miles (6,690km) with a full payload.

Accommodation: Flight crew of three, and up to 167 passengers.

Orders: Total of 154 built (65 720s and 89 720Bs).

Opposite top A 707 of Cathay Pacific takes off from its home base, Hong Kong. The 707 remains in production and is likely to overtake the DC-9 as the world's second-most popular jet. It is already easily the largest selling of all intercontinental and four-engined aircraft.
Left 'City of Geelong' one of the 707-338 fleet which was the backbone of the Qantas system before the arrival of the 747s. The 'V-Jet' symbol on the tail was retained for a time though replaced by a 'flying kangaroo' on the 747s. Qantas use their 707s on the relatively low density routes such as Sydney to Johannesburg, Tokyo, Mexico and Vancouver and also on the more crowded Australia—New Zealand routes.
Above An Ethiopian Airlines 720B, so similar to the 707 that it is sometimes designated 707-047B. The 720 was developed as a shorter fuselage, much lighter version of the 707 for American domestic routes, although a few strayed further afield.

Boeing 727

Short/medium-range airliner, operated throughout the world. The Boeing 727 has been sold in greater numbers than any other jet airliner. The original 727-100, first flown on February 9 1963, had seats for up to 131 passengers and entered service with three 14,000 pound (6,350kg) thrust JT8D-1 turbofans; more powerful JT8Ds quickly followed. Lengthened by 10ft (3·05m), the 727-200 can carry up to 189 passengers and has been fitted with progressively more powerful engines. The 727-100C and 200C are convertible cargo/passenger models; so are the 727-100QC and 200QC 'quick-change' aircraft, in which the passenger seats are mounted on pallets for rapid installation and removal.

Engines (current 727-200): Three Pratt & Whitney JT8D-15 turbofans, each giving 15,500 pounds (7,030kg) of thrust, in pods on each side of the rear fuselage and in the tailcone.

Maximum cruising speed (727-200/JT8D/15): 599mph (964km/h) at a height of 24,700ft (7,530m).

Typical range (727-200/JT8D-15): 1,845 miles (2,970km/h) with a full payload.

Accommodation (727-200): Flight crew of three, and up to 189 passengers.

Orders: Total of 1,166 of all versions sold, of which 1,068 had been delivered by 1974.

Boeing 737

Short-range airliner, initially operated by Lufthansa in 1968 and now throughout the world. The chubby appearance of the Boeing 737 results from the fact that its cabin cross-section is basically the same as that of the much longer 727 and 707. This fact, and the similarity of some items of equipment, help to keep both initial cost and servicing costs to a minimum. Even the engines are similar to those of the 727, although the 737 heralded the reversion to underwing pods. As in the case of the tri-jet, there is a basic 737-100 and a 'stretched' 737-200, with 'C' and 'QC' models of each for operators who want to carry both passengers and cargo.

Engines (current 737-200): Two Pratt & Whitney JT8D-15 turbofans, each giving 15,500 pounds (7,30kg) of thrust, in underwing pods.

Maximum cruising speed (737-200/JT8D-15): 576mph (927km/h) at a height of 22,600ft (6,890m).

Typical range (737-200/JT8D-15): 2,370 miles (3,815km) with 115 passengers.

Accommodation (737-200): Flight crew of two and up to 130 passengers.

Orders: Total of 415 sold (32 737-100s and 383 737-200s), of which 375 had been delivered by October 1 1974.

Top The first Boeing 727 acquired by Alia, the airline of Jordan, which is of the series 200 'stretched' variety. The 727 is the largest-selling jet airliner ever, and the only one of which there are over 1000 in service.
Bottom The Boeing fleet's 'baby', the 737, which has the same fuselage cross section as the 707 and 727. It differs from its main competitors—the DC-9, BAC1-11 and Caravelle—in having underwing rather than fuselage-mounted engines. This series 200 version is one of the eight which form the mainstay of the Air California fleet.

Boeing 747

Long-range large-capacity airliner, operated throughout the world. Boeing's famous 'Jumbo' flew for the first time on February 9 1969, and entered service on Pan American's New York/London route on January 22 1970. The largest capacity airliner in the world, and likely to remain so for the rest of the decade, the 747 is big enough to seat 500 passengers, though the aircraft used on intercontinental routes normally carry a maximum of about 360 at the present time. More powerful engines and increased operating weight distinguish the 747-200 from the basic 747-100. Variants are the convertible cargo/passenger 747C, the 747F freighter with upward-hinged nose loading door, the short-range 747SR with reduced weights, and the long-range 747SP with 48ft (14·63m) shorter fuselage. Nearly 73 million passengers had been carried by October 1 1974.

Engines (747-200): Four Pratt & Whitney JT9D-7A turbofans, each giving 46,150 pounds (20,950kg) of thrust, in underwing pods.

Maximum cruising speed (747-200): 608mph (978km/h) at a height of 30,000ft (9,150m).

Typical range (747-200): 4,330 miles (6,968km) with a full payload.

Accommodation (747-200): Flight crew of three or four, and up to 500 passengers.

Orders: Total of 277 sold of which 239 had been delivered by October 1 1974.

Main picture Over 300 tons of the world's largest aircraft on take-off from Dallas-Fort Worth. This was the only one of the type in use with Braniff up to 1975, working the lucrative Dallas-Honolulu run. Texas based Braniff, which has an intense series of routes linking North and South America, is unusual in having no single colour scheme. Instead it paints each plane in a distinctive colour, of which this 747 is not untypical.
Inset A 747 of Japan Air Lines lands at Tokyo's Haneda International Airport.

Canadair CL-44

Long-range passenger/freighter, operated primarily on charter flights from the UK and western Europe, and in South America and the Caribbean. By the beginning of 1975, only Cubana retained the original Britannia on passenger-carrying services and the only version to be found in regular service elsewhere was the Canadair CL-44. Evolved from the Britannia and first operating commercially in 1961, the CL-44 has a longer fuselage and different engines. Some are former Canadian military Yukons. Others are CL-44D4s, with a swing-tail which hinges to one side to permit straight-in loading of cargo into the rear fuselage. A few are CL-44Js, or Canadair 400s, with a 15ft (4·57m) longer fuselage that enabled their original owner, Loftleidir, to seat 214 passengers on transatlantic services.

Engines (CL-44D4): Four Rolls-Royce Tyne 515 turboprops, each rated at 5,730hp.

Maximum cruising speed (CL-44D4): 402 mph (647km/h) at a height of 21,000ft (6,400m).

Typical range (CL-44D4): 3,260 miles (5,245km) with 27½-ton payload.

Accommodation (CL-44D4): Flight crew of four, and freight or about 134 passengers.

Orders: A total of 39 CL-44s were built. Most continue in service.

Below A Cargolux Canadair 'City of Luxembourg' with the remarkable swing-tail which allows easy loading of freight. Despite the name of the airline and aircraft, and the use of Luxair facilities, Cargolux is actually an Icelandic airline and one of Flugleidir's many operational subsidiaries. 'City of Luxembourg' had previously operated passenger services for Loftleidir at a time when that airline based its advertizing policy on the fact that it was the only line flying the Atlantic and not using jets.

Inset above The Britannia in its prime, operating BOAC's trans-Atlantic services. The Canadair was developed from the Britannia in Canada and other examples of the type were still flying in 1975 with Transmeridian, Trans-Mediterranean, Aer Turas, Africargo and Cubana, the latter still operating passenger services.

Caravelle (Aerospatiale)

Medium-range airliner, operated throughout the world on scheduled and charter services. This jet airliner which first entered service in 1959, pioneered the idea of mounting podded engines on each side of the rear fuselage. This left the wing free of appendages and made the cabin much quieter than on other jets. Versions up to, and including, the Caravelle VI had Rolls-Royce Avon turbojets and up to 80 seats. The Super B, or 10B, was 40in (1m) longer, seating 104 persons, and introduced JT8D turbofan engines. Longest of all was the Caravelle 12, last of the line, with more powerful turbofans and up to 139 seats.

Engines (Caravelle 12): Two Pratt & Whitney JT8D-9 turbofans, each giving 14,500 pounds (6,577kg) of thrust, in pods on each side of the rear fuselage.

Maximum cruising speed (Caravelle 12): 512mph (825km/h) at a height of 25,000ft (7,620m).

Typical range (Caravelle 12): 1,580 miles (2,540km) with full payload.

Accommodation (Caravelle 12): Flight crew of two to four, and between 104 and 139 passengers.

Orders: A total of 280 Caravelles were built. About 230 remain in airline service.

This page Scandinavian Caravelle 'Sven Viking' prepares for take off. The flags of the three countries which operate SAS, Sweden, Norway and Denmark, can be seen on the engines. The Caravelle was the first jet to have engines mounted on the rear fuselage and is easily distinguishable from competitors by its slightly triangular windows and unusually-placed tail-plane.
Overleaf Night time at Paris-Orly for a selection of Air France Caravelles. In the foreground is one of the first of the series III models, 'Vercors'.

Comet 4 (Hawker Siddeley)

Medium-range airliner, operated only by Dan-Air on services from and within the UK, and by EgyptAir. Fewer than 20 Comet 4s remain in commercial service, to provide a direct link with the world's first jet airliner—the de Havilland (now part of Hawker Siddeley) Comet 1 of the early 1950s. They are a mixture of Comet 4Bs, with a span of 107ft 10in (32·87m) and length of 118ft (35·97m); and Comet 4Cs, with the same fuselage but wings of 114ft 10in (35m) span, carrying streamlined external pinion tanks on the leading-edges to increase fuel capacity.

Engines (Comet 4B): Four Rolls-Royce Avon 525 turbojets, each giving 10,500 pounds (4,760kg) of thrust, buried in the wing roots.

Maximum cruising speed (Comet 4B): 526mph (846km/h) at a height of 23,500ft (7,160m).

Typical range (Comet 4B): 3,120 miles (5,020km) with full payload.

Accommodation (Comet 4B): Flight crew of three and up to 101 passengers.

Orders: Total of 68 Comet 4 series were delivered for airline use. About 19 remained airworthy at the beginning of 1975.

Below Preparation for service at London's second airport, Gatwick, for one of the 17 Comet 4s still in service with Dan-Air in 1974. Developed from the Comet 1, the Comet 4 carved its own niche in aviation history by operating the first commercial transatlantic service, for BOAC (now British Airways), in October 1958. In fact the Comet was not really suited to the Atlantic route and Dan-Air, the only major operator by 1975, used them mainly for short range European charter work. It is unlikely that any will still be in passenger service by the beginning of 1976.

Concorde (Aerospatiale/BAC)

Medium/long-range supersonic airliner, scheduled to enter service in 1976. No more graceful or controversial aircraft than the Concorde has ever flown. Developed in partnership by the French and British aircraft industries, over a twelve-year period, at a cost of more than £1,000 million, it carries its passengers at twice the speed of sound. This enabled a Concorde to complete a return service from Boston, USA, to Paris, France, across the Atlantic, in the time taken by a Boeing 747 to make a one-way crossing. But its availability coincided with fuel and economic crises, and a new awareness of noise and smoke pollution which its designers had to work hard to satisfy. Full acceptance of supersonic airline flying is likely to come only when Concorde demonstrates its capabilities in service.

Engines: Four Rolls-Royce / SNECMA Olympus 593 Mk 602 turbojets, each giving 38,050 pounds (17,260kg) of thrust with reheat, paired in underwing ducts.

Maximum cruising speed: 1,354mph (2,179 km/h) at a height of 51,300ft (15,635m).

Typical range: 3,970 miles (6,380km) with full payload.

Accommodation: Flight crew of three and up to 128 passengers.

Orders: Firm orders of five for British Airways and four for Air France. CAAC of China and Iran Air plan to operate three each.

Left The prototype Concorde, which first flew on March 2 1969, some six years after its development began. The famous 'drooped' nose can be clearly seen.
Below One of the first production models of Concorde at the Aerospatiale plant in Toulouse. As these models were also used for sales exhibitions the other side of the aircraft would be painted in Air France colours.

Convair 990A Coronado

Medium/long-range airliner, operated on scheduled services by Swissair and on charter and inclusive-tour flights by Spantax of Spain and Modern Air Transport of the USA. Swissair plans to dispose of its Coronados in 1975. Fastest airliner currently in service, the Coronado can be distinguished by the four 'area-rule' conical fairings on the wing trailing-edges which rectified its initially disappointing performance. It was developed in the early 1960s, from the Convair 880, to meet the need of American Airlines for a transcontinental airliner. Its five-abreast seating made it more comfortable than the obvious competitors, the Boeing 707 and Douglas DC-8, but at the same time reduced its capacity and contributed to its failure. With the yet to be proven exception of the Concorde, the Coronado is widely regarded as the greatest commercial aircraft disaster ever—having reputedly lost Convair some $250 million. Most Coronados have now pas-

sed into service with charter operators.

Engines: Four General Electric CJ805-23B turbofans, each giving 16,000 pounds (7,280kg) of thrust, in underwing pods.

Maximum cruising speed: 615mph (990km/h) at a height of 20,000ft (6,100m).

Typical range: 3,800 miles (6,115km) with maximum fuel.

Accommodation: Flight crew of three to five, and up to 106 passengers.

Orders: A total of 37 Convair 990s were built, of which no more than 20 remain in service.

Dassault-Breguet Mercure

Short-range large-capacity airliner, operated by Air Inter mainly on domestic services between Paris and cities in France. Dassault decided to develop the Mercure as a private venture, to break into the worldwide market dominated by American 'twins' such as the Boeing 737. After a time the French government gave its financial support to the project and manufacturers in Italy, Spain, Belgium, Switzerland and Canada joined in, contributing to the cost in proportion to the amount of work they were allocated. Despite this, sales have been disappointing, with only one airline customer by the beginning of 1975.

Engines: Two Pratt & Whitney JT8D-15 turbofans, each giving 15,500 pounds (7,030kg) of thrust, in underwing pods.

Maximum cruising speed: 575mph (926km/h) at a height of 20,000ft (6,100m).

Typical range: 575 miles (925km) with 140 passengers.

Accommodation: Flight crew of two and up to 162 passengers.

Orders: Ten aircraft, for Air Inter, by the beginning of 1975.

Left *One of only seven Convair 990As remaining in scheduled service, all with Swissair, in 1974. Note the unusual conical fairings on the trailing edge of the wing.*
Above *Dassault-Breguet's direct competitor to the Boeing 737, the Mercure. The first models went into service on Air Inter's domestic routes from Paris in 1974.*

Douglas DC-3

Medium-range airliner in worldwide service, mainly for second-line and freight operations. One of the truly great aeroplanes of history, the DC-3 flew for the first time on December 22 1935 as the DST (14-passenger Douglas Sleeper Transport) and entered service in 1936. More than 10,000 were built for military use in World War II. Afterwards, many of these aircraft were made available to airlines, to supplement civil DC-3s, and most of the world's major operators rebuilt their network of services with these sturdy twins. More than 500 are believed to be still flying with airlines all over the world.

Engines: Two 1,200hp Pratt & Whitney R-1830-90C or -90D piston engines.
Maximum cruising speed: 198mph (318km/h) at a height of 6,000ft (1,830m).
Typical range: 1,510 miles (2,420km) with maximum fuel.
Accommodation: Flight crew of three and up to 36 passengers.
Orders: Altogether, 10,655 civil DC-3s and various military versions were built, a high proportion of which passed into airline service. In addition, a version known as the Lisunov Li-2 can still be seen in Russia, where it was built under licence.

Douglas DC-8

Long-range airliner, in worldwide service. First flown on May 30 1958, the initial DC-8 Srs 10 had 13,500 pound (6,124kg) thrust JT3C-6 turbojets and was intended for operation on American domestic routes. The Srs 20 was similar, with more powerful JT4A-3 engines; the Srs 30, 40 and 50 were designed for intercontinental operations, the last two with turbofans. All these versions were the same size. In 1965, Douglas intro-duced the Super 61, with fuselage lengthened by 36ft 8in (11·8m) to carry up to 259 passengers instead of the former 116 to 179. The Super 62 was only 6ft 8in (2·03m) longer than early models but was refined for very long range. The Super 63 combined the long fuselage of the 61 with the improvements of the 62. Cargo versions of the Srs 50 and the three Super DC-8s were sold as Jet Traders.

Engines: (Super 63): Four Pratt & Whitney JT3D-7 turbofans, each giving 19,000 pounds (8,618kg) of thrust, in underwing pods.
Maximum cruising speed (Super 63): 600mph (965km/h) at a height of 30,000ft (9,150m).
Typical range (Super 63): 4,500 miles (7,240km) with full payload.
Accommodation (Super 63): Flight crew of three to five and up to 259 passengers.
Orders: A total of 294 DC-8 Series 10 to 50 were built, plus 262 of the Super Sixty series. Of these more than 500 remained operational in 1975.

Below The most prolific airliner ever built— the Douglas DC-3, known by the RAF as the Dakota. Having entered service in 1936, several hundred were still in operation nearly 40 years later. This example is one of four operated by East African Airways at the beginning of 1975 and which is now numbered 5Y-AAE.
Right One of the 11 graceful DC-8-43s acquired by Alitalia for its medium distance routes. The airline also bought ten 'stretched' series 60s for larger capacity loads before the advent of the DC-10 and 747. In keeping with Alitalia's tradition of calling its larger aircraft after famous Italians, this example travels under the name 'Ugolino Vivaldi'.

Douglas DC-9

Short/medium-range airliner, in worldwide service. Best-selling short-range twin-jet airliner in the world, the DC-9 first flew on February 25 1965 and has since been built in five versions, with various models of the JT8D turbofan engine and with fuselages varying in length from 104ft 4¾in (31·82m) in the basic Srs 10 and 20 to 133ft 7¼in (40·72m) in the Srs 50 for use on high-density routes. There are all-cargo (DC-9F), quick-change passenger/cargo (DC-9CF) and mixed-traffic passenger/cargo (DC-9RC) versions of each series.

Engines (Srs 30): Two Pratt & Whitney JT8D-7 turbofans, each giving 14,000 pounds (6,350kg) of thrust, in pods on each side of the rear fuselage.

Maximum cruising speed (Srs 30): 565mph (909km/h) at a height of 25,000ft (7,620m).

Typical range (Srs 30): 1,725 miles (2,775km) with maximum fuel.

Accommodation (Srs 30): Flight crew of two and up to 115 passengers.

Orders: Total of 796 ordered of which more than 750 had been delivered by the beginning of 1975.

Main picture Trans-Australia Airlines' DC-9 'John Roe' on take-off from Melbourne's new Tullamarine Airport.

Inset left Another of TAA's fleet of 12 DC-9s, 'Angus McMillan', loading for a domestic flight and showing the slightly inclined nose which helps distinguish Douglas aircraft from those produced by Boeing.

Inset below Busy day at Kingston's Norman Manley International Airport. This provides an interesting comparison between the DC-8 series 50 at the top and the DC-8 series 60 at the bottom, the latter being able to take, at the extreme, nearly twice as many passengers as the former. The DC-8 series 60 was the ultimate in 'stretching' and could provide for up to 259 passengers in maximum high-density layout. Note the two DC-9s sandwiched between the DC-8s.

Douglas DC-1O

Medium/long-range large-capacity airliner, in service throughout the world. Like the TriStar, this three-turbofan airliner was designed originally to meet an American Airlines requirement for a large-capacity transport able to operate from smaller airports in the USA. From twin-engined projects, the designers switched eventually to three engines, with the third mounted uniquely above the fuselage at the base of the tail-fin. Initial versions are the basic Srs 10; the slightly larger Srs 30, with more powerful CF6 turbofans, for intercontinental routes; and the Srs 40, similar to the 30 but with Pratt & Whitney JT9D turbofans. There are DC-10CF convertible passenger/cargo versions of each,

and Douglas are planning new models, carrying cargo or up to 430 passengers. The airliner first entered commercial service in 1971.
Engines (Srs 30): Three General Electric CF6-50A turbofans, each giving 49,000 pounds (22,226kg) of thrust, two in underwing pods and the third in a pod at the base of the fin.
Maximum cruising speed (Srs 30): 578mph (930km/h) at a height of 30,000ft (9,145m).
Typical range (Srs 30): 4,375 miles (7,040km) with full payload.
Accommodation (Srs 30): Flight crew of three to five, and anything between 255 and 380 passengers.
Orders: Total of 215 firm orders for all versions, plus 40 options, by the beginning of 1975.

Main picture The first of the 16 DC-10s ordered by Continental Airlines of Los Angeles by the end of 1974.
Inset One of the DC-10-30s of UTA, France's second international airline.

Fokker-VFW F.27 Friendship

Short/medium-range airliner, in worldwide service. Most-produced turboprop airliner in history, the Friendship first flew in prototype form on November 24 1955, as a 28-passenger DC-3 replacement. The slightly longer Mk 100 initial production version, with 32 seats, was manufacturered by both Fokker in the Netherlands and Fairchild in the USA. Both companies subsequently produced 'stretched' versions, carrying up to 56 passengers, and with more powerful Dart turboprops. Freight versions were also introduced, with large cargo door at the front on the port side.

Engines (Mk 500): Two 2,140hp Rolls-Royce Dart Mk 532-7R turboprops.
Maximum cruising speed (Mk 500): 298mph (480km/h) at a height of 20,000ft (6,100m).
Typical range (Mk 500): 1,082 miles (1,741 km) with 52 passengers.
Accommodation (Mk 500): Flight crew of two to four, and up to 56 passengers.
Orders: Total of 621 orders including both Fokker and Fairchild versions.

Fokker-VFW F.28 Fellowship

Short-range airliner, in service in small numbers throughout the world, on local routes and for VIP transport. As in the case of many modern airliner projects, Fokker-VFW launched the Fellowship only after ensuring the support of its government (in this case the Netherlands government) and the cost-sharing assistance of other European manufacturers. Thus, the rear fuselage, tail unit and engine nacelles are produced in Germany, the wings by Shorts in Northern Ireland, and the engines by Rolls-Royce in England. The prototype F.28 Mk 1000 flew on May 9 1967, with up to 65 seats. The lengthened Mk 2000 carries up to 79 passengers. The Mks 5000 and 6000 are variants of the 1000 and 2000 respectively with longer-span, slatted wings to permit higher take-off weight with only slightly longer take-off runs.

Engines (Mk 2000): Two Rolls-Royce Spey Mk 555-15 turbofans, each giving 9,850 pounds (4,468kg) of thrust, in pods on each side of rear fuselage.
Maximum cruising speed (Mk 2000): 523mph (843km/h) at a height of 23,000ft (7,000m).
Typical range (Mk 2000): 806 miles (1,296 km) with 79 passengers.
Accommodation (Mk 2000): Flight crew of two and up to 79 passengers.
Orders: Total of 87 ordered by October 1 1974.

Fokker-VFW 614

Short-range airliner, under development in 1974. Like the Caravelle, the VFW 614 is pioneering an entirely new engine arrangement, this time with two turbofans mounted in pods above its wings. Work on the prototype began in 1968, with financial support from the German government, and cost-sharing participation in the programme by Fokker-VFW of the Netherlands, SABCA and Fairey of Belgium and MBB of Germany. The first of three prototypes flew on July 14 1971. Cimber Air placed the first firm order, for two, in April 1974. Another 24 are on option for airlines in Europe, the Philippines, the Argentine and Yemen. Operations by Cimber Air were scheduled to begin in mid-1975.

Engines: Two Roll-Royce/SNECMA M45H Mk 501 turbofans, each giving 7,280 pounds (3,302kg) of thrust, mounted in overwing pods.
Maximum cruising speed: 449mph (722km/h) at a height of 25,000ft (7,620m).
Typical range: 748 miles (1,205km) with 40 passengers.
Accommodation: Flight crew of two and up to 44 passengers.
Orders: Two for Cimber Air of Denmark, with options on 24 more.

Opposite top An F.27-200 of Ansett, one of Australia's two major domestic airlines. The F.27 was built in the United States under licence by Fairchild as the FH.227.
Opposite centre Fokker's jet successor to F.27 was the F.28, powered by two Rolls-Royce Spey engines. Garuda, the Indonesian airline which still has close links with KLM, took a number, one of which is shown.
Opposite bottom and below Developed in Germany rather than the Netherlands and therefore usually designated VFW-Fokker rather than Fokker-VFW (as the F.27 and F.28 are), the VFW 614 is due to go into service some time in 1975. It embodies a completely new design feature, that of overwing engine pods, clearly visible in both photographs.

Above A Hawker Siddeley 748 of Zambia Airways, known as the 'Eagle of Africa' and symbolized on the tail. Zambia uses its 748s on internal flights and to neighbouring countries such as Botswana and Malawi. Note the large cargo door behind the cockpit.
Right A Herald of British Island Airways, the main operator of the type. BIA uses them on all its services, the majority of which, as the line's title implies, are to the Channel Islands and the Isle of Man.

Hawker Siddeley 748

Short-range airliner, in service throughout the world. The HS748 is in the same size bracket as the Fokker-VFW Friendship and NAMC YS-11 and, like them, has Rolls-Royce Dart turboprop engines. Another feature shared with the YS-11 is that the engines are mounted **above** the wings. The original prototype flew on June 24 1960. Early aircraft were Srs 1s with 1,880hp Dart 514 engines. The Srs 2 and 2A differ in having 2,105hp Dart 531s and 2,280hp Dart 532-2s respectively.

Engines (Srs 2A): Two 2,280 hp Rolls-Royce Dart 532-2L or -2S turboprops.
Maximum cruising speed (Srs 2A): 278mph (448km/h) at a height of 10,000ft (3,050m).
Typical range (Srs 2A): 840 miles (1,351km) with full payload.
Accommodation: Flight crew of two and up to 58 passengers.
Orders: Total of 299 sold for military and commercial use including 69 assembled in India by Hindustan Aeronautics and 31 designated as Andovers by the Royal Air Force.

Herald (Handley Page)

Short-range airliner, in small-scale service on local routes in Europe, the Far East, Middle East, North and South America. Main operator is British Island Airways, with fourteen. Designed in the 1950s by the famous Handley Page company, which was registered in 1909, the Herald was flown originally with four Leonides Major piston-engines. It was soon clear that potential customers preferred turboprops, so the prototypes were re-engined with two Darts and this version went into production as the 44-seat Herald Srs 100. After a short time, it was superseded by the Srs 200, with 56 seats in a 42in (1·07m) longer fuselage; but the Herald could not survive against competition from the Friendship and HS748, although most of those built continue to give good service.

Engines: Two 2,105hp Rolls-Royce Dart 527 turboprops.

Maximum cruising speed (Srs 200): 275mph (442km/h) at 15,000ft (4,575m).

Typical range (Srs 200): 700 miles (1,125km) with full payload.

Accommodation (Srs 200): Flight crew of three and up to 56 passengers.

Orders: Total of 37 delivered for commercial use. About 31 continue airworthy. Users include Arkia, British Air Ferries, British Island Airways and British Midland Airways.

Ilyushin IL-18

Medium-range turboprop airliner, in service on many Aeroflot routes and, in small numbers, in Africa, eastern Europe, China and Cuba. Most successful modern Soviet airliner, in terms of exports, the Il-18 was evolved to replace a variety of earlier piston-engined transports. The first 20 aircraft, flown in the late 1950s, were fitted with either Kuznetsov NK-4 or Ivchenko AI-20 turboprops; the latter became standard from number 21. Seats for 84 passengers were provided initially, but production centred primarily on the Il-18V with 90 to 110 seats. Variants were the Il-18E with 4,250hp engines and 110-122 seats; and the Il-18D, similar except for having extra fuel tanks.

Engines (Il-18V): Four 4,000hp Ivchenko AI-20K turboprops.

Maximum cruising speed (Il-18V): 404mph (650km/h) at a height of 26,250ft (8,000m).

Typical range (Il-18V): 1,553 miles (2,500km) with full payload.

Accommodation (Il-18V): Flight crew of four or five and up to 110 passengers.

Orders: Production is believed to exceed 700, mainly for Aeroflot. More than 100 were exported for military and civil use, major operators in 1974 including Balkan Bulgarian Airlines with nine, CAAC of China with nine, CSA of Czechoslovakia with seven, Interflug of East Germany with 14, LOT of Poland with eight, and Tarom of Rumania with 11.

Ilyushin IL-62

Long-range jet airliner, used on Aeroflot's longer routes and in small numbers by airlines in eastern Europe, Egypt and China. Similar in layout to Britain's VC10, the Il-62 was developed to replace the big turboprop Tu-114 on Aeroflot routes to places like New York, Montreal, Tokyo and Cuba. The prototype flew in January 1963, with turbojets installed temporarily. Production Il-62s, with Kuznetsov NK-8-4 turbofans and standard seating for 168 passengers, did not enter service until 1967. They are being followed and possibly replaced, by the improved Il-62M, with different engines and up to 186 seats but no change in overall dimensions.

Engines (Il-62M): Four Soloviev D-30KU turbofans, each giving 25,350 pounds (11,500kg) of thrust, mounted in pairs in pods on each side of rear fuselage.

Maximum cruising speed (Il-62M): 560mph (900km/h) at a height of 39,400 ft (12,000m).

Typical range (Il-62M): 4,970 miles (8,000 km) with full payload.

Accommodation (Il-62M): Flight crew of five and up to 186 passengers.

Orders: About 50 Il-62s and Il-62Ms had been delivered to Aeroflot by mid-1974. The Il-62Ms are being used initially on the airline's Moscow-Havana route; eventually there will be sufficient to operate all its very long-distance services. About 30 Il-62s have been delivered so far to other airlines.

Opposite page Aeroflot Ilyushin Il-18s crowd
the tarmac at Moscow's Domodedovo
Airport on a typically Russian winter's day.
Below More inclement weather to be faced by
one of Aeroflot's several hundred Il-18s.
Bottom Shades of the VC-10 in this Interflug
Ilyushin Il-62, the only other jet airliner
powered by four rear-mounted engines.

Lockheed Electra

Medium-range turboprop airliner, used on both passenger and cargo services, mainly in North, Central and South America, and in Australasia. The Electra, which first entered commercial service early in 1959, was intended as America's second-generation follow-up to the Viscount, following the latter type's successful invasion of the American market in the 1950s. Like the Vanguard, it arrived just as airlines began the switch to turbojet types, and it was ordered in much smaller numbers than had been anticipated. Many of those that remain have been fitted with a large freight door at the front of the cabin on the port side.

Engines: Four 3,750hp Allison 501-D13 turboprops.

Maximum cruising speed: 405mph (652km/h) at a height of 22,000ft (6,700m).

Typical range: 2,500 miles (4,020km) with a payload of nearly ten tons.

Accommodation: Flight crew of three or four, and up to 99 passengers.

Orders: A total of 165 Electras were ordered by 14 airlines. More than 100 continue in service.

Lockheed TriStar

Medium/long-range large-capacity airliner, operated on trunk routes and charter services in the USA, Canada, Japan, the Middle East, and from the UK and Germany. Lockheed's counterpart to the DC-10 has had a chequered career. Its first flight, on November 16 1970, coincided with the collapse and subsequent government take-over of Rolls-Royce, maker of its engines. Lockheed itself had financial problems, and sales of the TriStar were slow as potential customers wondered about the future of the project. Not until passenger services by Eastern Air Lines began in April 1972 did the quality of both aircraft and engines begin to overcome the hesitancy. The basic L-1011 TriStar is now to be followed by the L-1011-200, with 48,000 pound (21,772 kg) thrust RB.211-524 engines and fuel for a range of more than 4,000 miles (6,440km).

Engines (L-1011): Three Rolls-Royce RB. 211-22B turbofans, each giving 42,000 pounds (19,050kg) of thrust; two in underwing pods and the third in the fuselage tailcone.

Maximum cruising speed (L-1011): 560mph (901km/h) at a height of 35,000ft (10,670m).

Typical range (L-1011): 2,677 miles (4,308 km) with full payload.

Accommodation: Flight crew of three to five, and between 256 and 400 passengers.

Orders: Total of 139 firm orders, plus options on 62 more by the beginning of 1975.

NAMC YS-11

Short/medium-range turboprop airliner, operated throughout the world. Most of the major aircraft manufacturing companies in Japan pooled their resources to build that nation's first post-war airliner. The Nihon Aeroplane Manufacturing Company (NAMC) was formed to undertake responsibility for design and to control production and sales. The prototype, which flew on August 30 1962, proved to be larger and more powerful than its European competitors. The basic YS-11-100 was followed by the YS-11A series with the same dimensions and power plant but increased payload. The YS-11-100, YS-11A-200 and -500 are all 60-seaters. The YS-11A-300 and -600 carry a mixture of 46 passengers and cargo. The YS-11A-400 is an all-cargo model.

Engines: Two 3,060hp Rolls-Royce Dart Mk 542-10K turboprops.

Maximum cruising speed (YS-11A-200): 291mph (469km/h) at a height of 15,000ft (4,575m).

Typical range (YS-11A-200): 680 miles (1,090km) with full payload.

Accommodation (YS-11A-200): Flight crew of two and up to 60 passengers.

Orders: Total of 182 built including 23 for the Japan Self-Defence Forces.

Below An NAMC YS-11 of Transair, a Canadian company based in Winnipeg. The type, very similar in appearance to the Hawker Siddeley 748, is rare in Europe and North America.

Nord 262 (Aerospatiale)

Short-range airliner, operated worldwide on local services. This light transport began life in 1959 as the Max Holste MH-250 Super Broussard, with a boxy unpressurized fuselage and two Wasp piston-engines. It was taken over by Nord Aviation, which built a pre-production batch of ten Nord 260s with Bastan turboprops and a longer fuselage. Nord then evolved a pressurized version, known as the Nord 262, with a circular-section fuselage. With uprated engines this is now produced as the civil and military Frégate by Aérospatiale, the French national company which absorbed Nord-Aviation in 1970.

Engines: Two 1,145hp Turboméca Bastan VII turboprops.
Maximum cruising speed: 254mph (408 km/h).
Typical range: 633 miles (1,020km) with 26 passengers.
Accommodation: Flight crew of two, and 26 or 29 passengers.
Orders: About 39 bought for airline service, largest single contract being 12 for Lake Central (now Allegheny) in the USA. Other operators include Rousseau of France and Cimber Air of Denmark.

Skyvan, Skyliner and SD3-30 (Shorts)

General-purpose light short take-off and landing transports, used throughout the world for local passenger and freight traffic, particularly where paved airfields are small or non-existent. Launched by Shorts as a private venture in 1959, the Skyvan was conceived as a STOL (short take-off and landing) aircraft with a box-like cabin, able to carry a two-ton load of passengers, cargo or anything else not too big to enter via its rear loading ramp. The original piston-engines of the prototype were replaced quickly with Astazou turboprops. Sixteen Skyvan 2s were then built with Astazous before the Skyvan 3 appeared as the main production version with AiResearch engines. Military and civil orders began to arrive at a respectable rate, and a new version named the Skyliner offered such superior furnishings that the King of Nepal bought one as a VIP transport. In 1974 came the first flight of the SD3-30, a largely re-engineered and 'stretched' version of the Skyliner which is 12ft longer and seats up to 30 passengers. Due to enter service in 1976, the first orders had been received nearly two years earlier from Command Airways of New York and Time Air of Calgary.

Engines (Srs 3ie Skyvan 3): Two 715hp AiResearch TPE 331-201 turboprops.
Maximum cruising speed (Srs 3): 203mph (327km/h) at a height of 10,000ft (3,050m).
Typical range (Srs 3): 694 miles (1,115km) with maximum fuel.
Accommodation (Srs 3): Flight crew of one or two. Up to 19 passengers, or 4,600 pounds (2,085kg) of cargo.
Orders: Total of 103 orders including 47 for military use by the end of 1974.

Opposite top One of the four Nord 262s operated by the Danish company Cimber Air.
Opposite bottom One of the box-like Skyliners used by the Scottish Regional division of British Airways for their island services out of Glasgow.
Below The prototype SD3-30 which Shorts have developed from the Skyliner.

Trident (Hawker Siddeley)

Short/medium-range airliner, operated mainly by the European Division of British Airways and CAAC of China. Others flown by the airlines of Iraq, Cyprus and Sri Lanka. This elegant three-turbofan airliner was designed to meet BEA's requirement for a 600mph short-range transport for its European services from 1963. The first of 24 Trident 1s for this airline flew on January 9 1962, with up to 103 seats, 9,850 pound (4,468kg) thrust Spey 505 engines and span of 89ft 10in (27·38m). Other companies ordered slightly larger and more powerful Trident 1Es, with up to 115 seats. BEA followed with an order for 15 Trident Twos (2Es), with increased span and power, and 26 Trident Threes (3Bs), with an added turbojet engine in the tailcone to boost performance from 'hot or high' airfields, with 128 to 180 passengers on board. CAAC, having acquired four Trident 1Es from Pakistan, decided to buy 33 new 2Es and an initial batch of two longer-range Super Trident 3Bs.

Engines (Trident Three): Three Rolls-Royce Spey Mk 512-5W turbofans, each giving 11,960 pounds (5,425kg) of thrust; two

mounted in pods on each side of rear fuselage and one in fuselage tailcone. One Rolls-Royce RB.162-86 auxiliary turbojet, giving 5,250 pounds (2,381kg) of thrust, above rear engine nozzle.

Maximum cruising speed (Trident Three): 601mph (967km/h) at a height of 28,300ft (8,625m).

Typical range (Trident Three): 1,094 miles (1,760km) with full payload.

Accommodation (Trident Three): Flight crew of three or four, and up to 180 passengers.

Orders: Total of 117 ordered by the end of 1974.

Both pictures Two different views of the first Trident 2E delivered by Hawker Siddeley to the Civil Aviation Administration of China (CAAC). This particular model was wheeled out in October 1972, being the first of 33 for mainland China. Note the 'reversed' Chinese flag on the tail, standard practice on the starboard side of aircraft.

Tupolev Tu-134

Short/medium-range airliner, operated mainly by Aeroflot on domestic services within the Soviet Union. Export sales have been made exclusively to airlines in eastern Europe and the Balkan states. Following the success achieved by its twin-jet Tu-104, first jet airliner in the world after the Comet 1, Tupolev scaled down the design to produce the 56-seat twin-turbofan Tu-124. This was intended to become the most widely-used aircraft on Aeroflot's short/medium routes. Instead, Tupolev switched production to the much-improved rear-engined T-tail Tu-134, which had been evolved originally under the designation Tu-124A. Versions are the basic 64/72-passenger Tu-134, and the lengthened Tu-134A with 76-80 seats, thrust reversers on the engines and improved equipment. Either version can have a glazed nose or conical radome.

Engines (Tu-134A): Two Soloviev D-30-2 turbofans, each giving 14,990 pounds (6,800kg) of thrust, in pods on each side of rear fuselage.

Maximum cruising speed (Tu-134A): 550mph (885km/h) at a height of 32,800ft (10,000m).

Typical range (Tu-134A): 1,081 miles (1,740 km) with full payload.

Accommodation (Tu-134A): Flight crew of three and up to 80 passengers.

Orders: Total of more than 225 built by October 1974, at least 150 for Aeroflot and the others for airlines in eastern Europe and the Balkans.

Tupolev Tu-144

Medium/long-range supersonic airliner, scheduled to enter service in 1975. The production version of Russia's supersonic airliner has undergone drastic design changes by comparison with the prototypes. The 'double-delta' wing is now cambered from root to tip; the engines are paired in separate ducts, which entailed complete redesign of the undercarriage; and retractable 'moustache' foreplanes have been added to improve take-off and landing performance. Except for the foreplanes, the changes make it more like Concorde; but the Tu-144 is a larger aircraft, intended to carry more people at a higher cruising speed. The prototype was the first supersonic airliner to fly, on the last day of 1968. It was also the first airliner to exceed Mach 1 and Mach 2; and four production Tu-144s began proving flights with mail and freight in 1974.

Engines: Four Kuznetsov NK-144 turbofans, each giving 44,090 pounds (20,000kg) of thrust with reheat, paired in underwing ducts.

Maximum cruising speed: 1,550mph (2,500 km/h) at a height of 52,500ft (16,000m).

Typical range: 4,030 miles (6,500km) with maximum fuel, carrying 140 passengers, at 1,243mph (2,000km/h).

Accommodation: Flight crew of three and up to 140 passengers.

Orders: Aeroflot is believed to require about 30 Tu-144s initially. CSA of Czechoslovakia has expressed a requirement for four.

Tupolev Tu-154

Medium/long-range airliner, in service on many Aeroflot domestic and international routes. Exported to several countries in eastern Europe and the Balkans. Intended to replace the Tu-104 and the turboprop Il-18 and An-10 on Aeroflot routes, the Tu-154 is the most refined subsonic airliner yet produced in Russia. The prototype made its first flight on October 4 1968. Regular passenger-carrying operations began in early 1972, and well over 100 Tu-154s were reported to be flying with Aeroflot by the spring of 1974. The Tupolev design team is said to be developing an improved version, known as the Tu-154A. Dimensionally unchanged, this is believed to have Soloviev D-30KU turbofans, rated at 25,350 pounds (11,500kg) thrust, seats for up to 175 passengers and a full-payload range of more than 3,000 miles (4,800km).

Engines (Tu-154): Three Kuznetsov NK-8-2 turbofans, each giving 20,950 pounds (9,500kg) of thrust; two mounted in pods on each side of the rear fuselage, the third inside the tailcone.

Maximum cruising speed (Tu-154): 605mph (975km/h) at a height of 31,150ft (9,500m).

Typical range (Tu-154): 3,977 miles (6,400 km) with 95 passengers.

Accommodation (Tu-154): Flight crew of three or four, and up to 167 passengers.

Orders: In addition to the very large quantity required by Aeroflot, 25 Tu-154s have been ordered by or delivered to Balkan Bulgarian Airlines, Malev, EgyptAir, Aviogenex of Jugoslavia and CSA of Czechoslovakia.

Opposite top A Tupolev Tu-134 of Aeroflot.
Opposite bottom The Tu-144, likely to be the first supersonic airliner in passenger service.
Below A Tu-154 coming in to land.

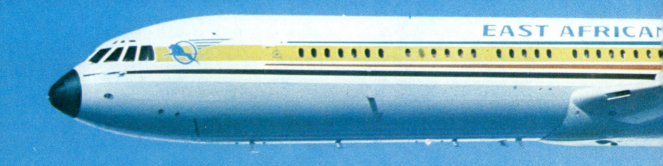

VC10 (Vickers/BAC)

Medium/long-range airliners, operated on British Airways Overseas Division services from UK, and by airlines in Africa and the Middle East. The VC10, which first entered commercial service in 1964, was evolved as the airliner likely to restore Britain to the front rank among designers of long-distance commercial transports. BOAC (now British Airways) expected to operate it almost exclusively over the old Empire routes, with their 'hot and high' airfields; eventually the design progressed so well that Vickers was able to offer transatlantic capability. In the end, however, BOAC bought only 12 VC10s and 17 of the 'stretched', longer-range Super VC10s. Today, British Airways operates

16 Supers; other operators of the two versions include East African Airways, Ghana Airways, Gulf Air and Air Malawi. Other than the Il-62, the VC10 is the only airliner operating with four rear-mounted engines.

Engines (Super VC10): four Rolls-Royce Conway 550 turbofans, each giving 22,500 pounds (10,205kg) of thrust, mounted in pairs in pods on the sides of the rear fuselage.

Maximum cruising speed (Super VC10): 568mph (914km/h) at a height of 38,000ft (12,460m).

Typical range (Super VC10): 4,630 miles (7,450km) with full payload.

Accommodation (Super VC10): Flight crew of three to five, and up to 174 passengers.

Orders: Total of 18 VC10s and 22 Super VC10s delivered to airlines.

Main picture *A Super VC-10 in the colours of East African Airways, the national airline of Kenya, Tanzania and Uganda.*
Inset *An unusual angle on one of BOAC's (now British Airways) fleet of VC10s, the inspiration of its famous 'try a little VC10derness' advertizing campaign. A remarkable aircraft, the VC10 was the only non-Russian jet built with four rear-mounted engines and also had a longer range, at full payload, than any of its competitors. Nevertheless, it never broke out of the traditional British markets and failed to penetrate either mainland Europe or the United States.*

Vanguard (Vickers)

Short/medium-range airliner, operated by the European Division of British Airways (mainly on cargo services), and by Invicta International Airlines of UK, Europe Aero Service of France and Merpati of Indonesia. This 'big brother' of the Viscount came on the scene too late to match the worldwide success of that pioneer British turboprop transport. The prototype flew on January 20 1959, followed by the first of 20 Vanguard 951s and higher-weight 953s for BEA only three months later. These aircraft gave superb service, as did the slightly more powerful Vanguard 952s bought by TCA (later Air Canada), but were outpaced by contemporary jets. Nine of the 13 remaining BEA Vanguards have been converted into Merchantman freighters and are now operated by British Airways.

Engines (Vanguard 952): Four 5,545hp Rolls-Royce Tyne 512 turboprops.
Maximum cruising speed (952): 425mph (684km/h) at a height of 20,000ft (6,100m).
Typical range (952): 1,830 miles (2,945km) with full payload.
Accommodation (952): Flight crew of three or four, and between 76 and 139 passengers.
Orders: Total of 43 built, of which about 28 remain airworthy.

Viscount (Vickers)

Short/medium-range turboprop airliner. Most major airlines have retired the majority, or all, of their former large fleets of Viscounts, but British Airways' Regional Division still has over 30 and British Midland Airways a dozen. Others can be seen throughout the world on local airline, charter and executive duties. First flown in prototype form on July 16 1948, the Viscount entered service with BEA in April 1953, to operate the world's first turboprop scheduled flights. With no competition, the Viscount attracted worldwide sales, even in the USA, and was produced in a bewildering succession of versions, with successively higher-powered Dart engines and greater payloads. Production finally ended in the spring of 1964, the last order being six for CAAC of China.

Engines (Viscount 810): Four 1,990hp Rolls-Royce Dart 525 turboprops.
Maximum cruising speed (810): 358mph (576km/h) at a height of 15,000ft (4,575m).
Typical range (810): 1,760 miles (2,830km) with 6½-ton payload.
Accommodation (810): Flight crew of three or four, and between 52 and 75 passengers.
Orders: Total of 444 built (for 48 airlines, 5 governments and 7 private owners in 40 countries). About 130 remained in airline service at the beginning of 1975.

Yakovlev Yak-40

Short-range airliner, operated over numerous local-service routes in Russia, and in small numbers by airlines in West Germany, Afghanistan and elsewhere. Smallest of the current range of jet airliners produced in the Soviet Union, the Yak-40 was given three engines to ensure good take-off performance on small, unprepared airfields. All three turbofans normally run at cruise power in flight, but it can, in fact, take off on two and cruise on only one engine. The prototype flew for the first time on October 21 1966. Passenger services began in September 1968, and Yak-40s had carried more than eight million passengers in Aeroflot operations by the spring of 1973. Versions include air ambulances and executive transports; a freighter is under development.

Engines: Three Ivchenko AI-25 turbofans, each giving 3,300 pounds (1,500kg) of thrust, mounted in pods on each side of rear fuselage and in fuselage tailcone.
Maximum cruising speed: 342mph (550km/h) at a height of 23,000ft (7,000m).
Typical range: 1,118 miles (1,800km) with full payload.
Accommodation: Flight crew of two and about 30 passengers in standard airline versions.
Orders: More than 400 had been built by the spring of 1973, mainly for Aeroflot. At least 100 more were scheduled for completion at that time.

Opposite top A Merchantman of British Airways European Division taxi-ing out at Glasgow's Abbotsinch Airport. The Merchantman is a Vanguard converted solely for cargo work and is one of the few remaining examples of the type still at work. In 1975 Merpati of Indonesia still had five operating passenger services, but it is unlikely that the Vanguard will still be carrying passengers on its twentieth birthday in 1979.
Opposite bottom The highly successful short-range Yakovlev Yak-40.
Previous pages A Viscount of British Midland Airways on the tarmac at Castle Donnington Airport, near Derby.

The world's major passenger airlines

Aer Lingus-Irish International Airlines
(Aer Lingus Teoranta)

Head office: PO Box 180, Dublin Airport, Eire.
Founded: 1936.
Routes: In conjunction with Aerlinte Eireann (founded 1947) a network of regional services and international routes is operated from Dublin, Shannon and Cork, principally to New York, Boston, Chicago, Montreal, London, Manchester, Glasgow, Paris, Amsterdam, Copenhagen, Frankfurt, Brussels, Zurich, Geneva, Rome and Madrid.
Aircraft operated: Boeing 707, 737, 747.

Left A Boeing 707 in the new green-toned livery of Aer Lingus. The symbol on the tail represents the shamrock. The airline usually called Aer Lingus actually comprises Aerlinte Eireann (basically intercontinental and coded by IATA as IN) and Aer Lingus Teoranta (handling European traffic and coded EI) but the two, to all intents and purposes, operate as one. This arrangement means, however, that Aer Lingus is one of very few airlines (British Airways, Flugleidir, the Ansett Group and tiny Air Illinois are the others) to bask in more than one IATA booking code.
Below The insignia of Aeroflot.

Aeroflot

Head office: Leningradsky Prospekt 37, Moscow A-167, USSR.
Founded: Formed originally as the government-owned Dobroflot under the first Five Year Plan of 1928, and subsequently taking over the private airline companies. The name Aeroflot was adopted during the re-organization of 1932.
Routes: The world's largest airline, Aeroflot operates an extensive domestic network and provides international services to Europe, Africa, Asia, Cuba, Canada and the USA, with further expansion planned. Other non-passenger activities include survey, agricultural and aero-medical services.
Aircraft operated: An-2, An-12, An-22, An-24; Il-18, Il-62, Il-76, Il-86; L-410; Polish-Soviet M-15; Tu-104, Tu-144, Tu-114, Tu-124, Tu-134, Tu-154, Tu-154A; Yak-40, Yak-18T. Helicopters in service are mainly Ka-26; Mil Mi-1, Mi-4, Mi-6/10, Mi-8; also some Il-14; An-14 and Yak-12.

Aerolineas Argentinas
Aeromexico

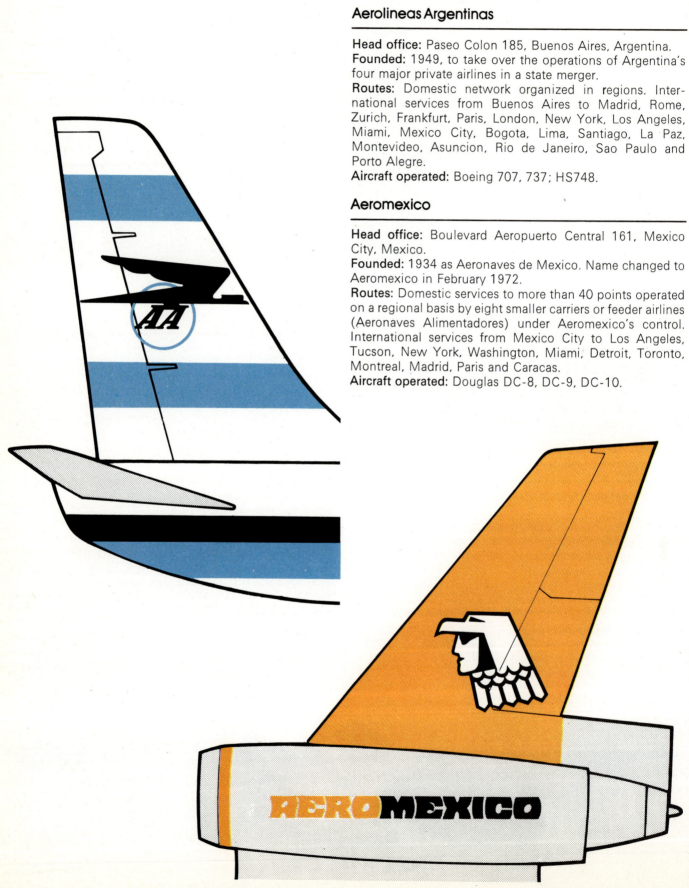

Aerolineas Argentinas

Head office: Paseo Colon 185, Buenos Aires, Argentina.
Founded: 1949, to take over the operations of Argentina's four major private airlines in a state merger.
Routes: Domestic network organized in regions. International services from Buenos Aires to Madrid, Rome, Zurich, Frankfurt, Paris, London, New York, Los Angeles, Miami, Mexico City, Bogota, Lima, Santiago, La Paz, Montevideo, Asuncion, Rio de Janeiro, Sao Paulo and Porto Alegre.
Aircraft operated: Boeing 707, 737; HS748.

Aeromexico

Head office: Boulevard Aeropuerto Central 161, Mexico City, Mexico.
Founded: 1934 as Aeronaves de Mexico. Name changed to Aeromexico in February 1972.
Routes: Domestic services to more than 40 points operated on a regional basis by eight smaller carriers or feeder airlines (Aeronaves Alimentadores) under Aeromexico's control. International services from Mexico City to Los Angeles, Tucson, New York, Washington, Miami, Detroit, Toronto, Montreal, Madrid, Paris and Caracas.
Aircraft operated: Douglas DC-8, DC-9, DC-10.

Air Afrique (Societe Aerienne Africaine Multinationale)

Head office: PO Box 21017, Abidjan, Ivory Coast.
Founded: 1961, under an agreement between 11 former French colonies, Cameroon (now withdrawn); Central African Republic; Congo-Brazzaville; Ivory Coast; Dahomey; Gabon; Upper Volta; Mauretania; Niger; Senegal; and Chad, (Togo joined later in 1968), and the Societe pour le Development du Transport Aerien en Afrique (Sodetraf).
Routes: Internal services to cover 22 African states. International services to Bordeaux, Lyon, Marseille, Paris, Nice, Geneva, Zurich, Rome, Las Palmas and New York.
Aircraft operated: Douglas DC-3, DC-8, DC-10; Caravelle.

Opposite top The tail of a 737 of Argentina's premier airline, Aerolineas Argentinas.
Opposite bottom Aeromexico's Aztec insignia adorns the tails of its DC-10s. As Aeronaves the airline was once a subsidiary of Pan Am.
Left The tail of a DC-8, operated by Air Afrique on its European services.
Below The tail of a Boeing 737 of another airline with French connections, Air Algerie.

Air Algerie (Compagnie Nationale de Transport Aerien)

Head office: 1 Place Maurice Audin, Algiers, Algeria.
Founded: 1953.
Routes: Extensive domestic network linking new cities and remote settlements with Algiers and Oran. International services to points in North and West Africa, France, Belgium, Spain, Italy, Germany, Switzerland, Egypt, Jugoslavia, Bulgaria, UK, Libya, Czechoslovakia, USSR and the Balearic Islands. Also extensive charter operations to both on-line and off-line points.
Aircraft operated: Boeing 727, 737; Caravelle; Convair CV-640.

Air California

Head office: 3636 Birch Street, Newport Beach, California 92660, USA.
Founded: 1966.
Routes: High frequency intra-state passenger services between Orange County—Disneyland, San·Francisco, San Diego, Oakland, San Jose, Palm Springs, Sacramento and Ontario.
Aircraft operated: Boeing 737; Lockheed Electra.

Air Canada

Head office: 1 Place Ville Marie, Montreal PQ, Canada.
Founded: 1937, as Trans-Canada Air Lines. Name changed to Air Canada in 1964.
Routes: Domestic transcontinental services linking major centres. International services to Europe, USA, Bermuda, the Caribbean and the Bahamas.
Aircraft operated: Boeing 727, 747; Douglas DC-8, DC-9; TriStar; Viscount.

Air Ceylon

Head office: PO Box 692, Lower Chatham Street, Colombo, Sri Lanka.
Founded: 1947, as Ceylon Airways Limited. Name changed to Air Ceylon in the following year.
Routes: Domestic services from Colombo to Jaffna, Trincomalee, Batticaloa and Gal Oya. International services from Colombo to Bombay, Madras, Tiruchirapalli, Karachi, London, Rome, Singapore, Kuala Lumpur, Bangkok, Paris.
Aircraft operated: Douglas DC-8, DC-3; Trident One; HS748.

Previous pages An Air Canada Boeing 727.
Top left The insignia of Air Ceylon, national airline of Sri Lanka.
Centre left The 'Sunshine' tail of a Boeing 737 of intra-state operator Air California.
Below A Douglas DC-9 of Canada's premier airline. The insignia on the tail represents Canada's national symbol, the Maple Leaf.

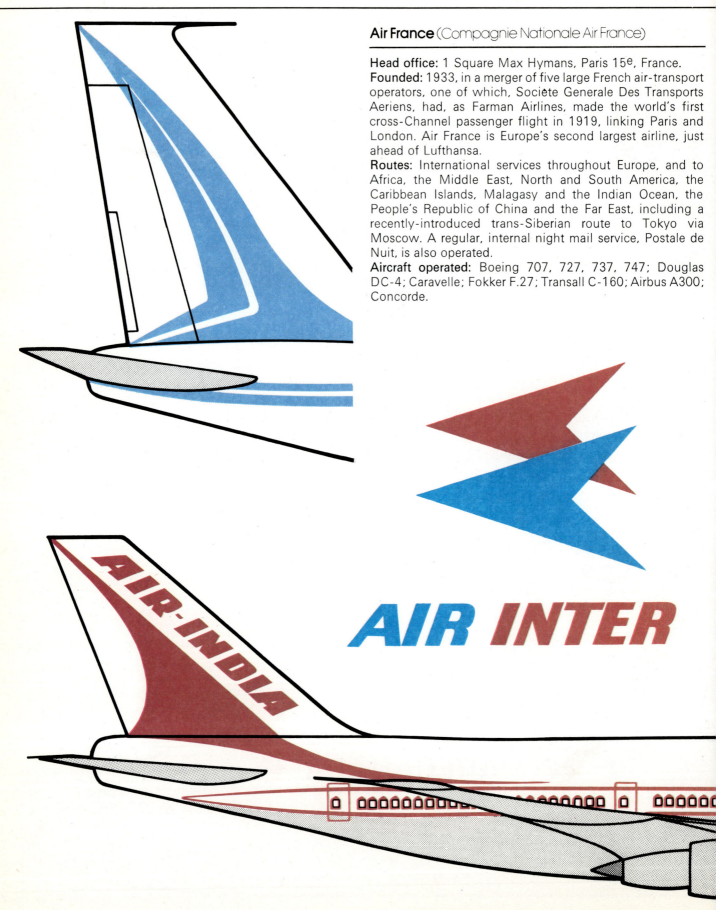

Air France (Compagnie Nationale Air France)

Head office: 1 Square Max Hymans, Paris 15e, France.

Founded: 1933, in a merger of five large French air-transport operators, one of which, Société Generale Des Transports Aeriens, had, as Farman Airlines, made the world's first cross-Channel passenger flight in 1919, linking Paris and London. Air France is Europe's second largest airline, just ahead of Lufthansa.

Routes: International services throughout Europe, and to Africa, the Middle East, North and South America, the Caribbean Islands, Malagasy and the Indian Ocean, the People's Republic of China and the Far East, including a recently-introduced trans-Siberian route to Tokyo via Moscow. A regular, internal night mail service, Postale de Nuit, is also operated.

Aircraft operated: Boeing 707, 727, 737, 747; Douglas DC-4; Caravelle; Fokker F.27; Transall C-160; Airbus A300; Concorde.

Air Inter (Lignes Aeriennes Interieures)

Head office: 232 Rue de Rivoli, Paris 1, France.
Founded: 1954, to meet provincial demands for internal air services within metropolitan France.
Routes: Extensive domestic network between Paris and most major cities in France.
Aircraft operated: Caravelle; Viscount; Fokker F.27; Dassault Mercure.

Opposite top left The tail of a Boeing 707 of Air France, Europe's second largest airline.
Opposite right The insignia of France's domestic airline, Air Inter.
Above The same insignia, displayed on a Fokker F.27. Air Inter purchased ten of these aircraft for use on short distance routes such as Marseilles—Toulouse or Lyon—Bordeaux.

Air-India

Head office: Air-India Building, 218 Backbay Reclamation, Nariman Point, Bombay 1, India.
Founded: 1948.
Routes: International services from Bombay, Calcutta and Delhi to Europe, Africa, the Far and Middle East, the USA and Australia.
Aircraft operated: Boeing 747 and 707.

Below A Boeing 747 of Air India, that country's international carrier. Air India initially bought four of the type to operate its Bombay—London—New York route.

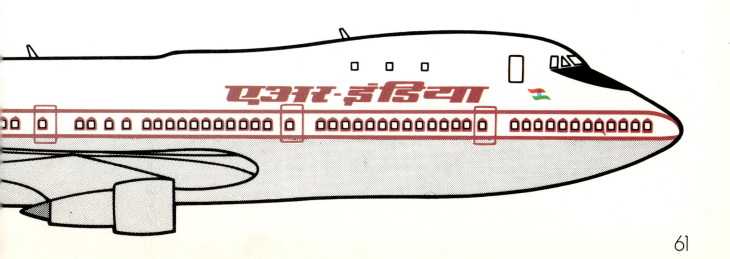

Air Jamaica
Air Madagascar (Societe Nationale Malagache de Transports Aeriens)

Air Jamaica

Head office: 72–76 Harbour Street, Kingston, Jamaica.
Founded: 1968, by Jamaican Government (60 percent shareholding) and Air Canada (40 percent), with the latter providing initial management and technical assistance.
Routes: International service linking Kingston and Montego Bay with New York, Miami, Chicago, Philadelphia, Toronto, Nassau, Detroit and London.
Aircraft operated: Douglas DC-9 and DC-8.

Air Madagascar (Societe Nationale Malagache de Transports Aeriens)

Head office: 31 Avenue de l'Independence, Tananarive, Malagasy.
Founded: 1962.
Routes: Extensive domestic network radiating from Tananarive plus regional services to Nairobi, Dar-es-Salaam, Lourenco Marques, Johannesburg, the Comoro Islands and Reunion. Intercontinental services to Paris, Marseille and Rome via Djibouti.
Aircraft operated: Boeing 707, 737; Douglas DC-4, DC-3; Nord 262; Twin Otter; Navajo; Aztec; Cherokee Six.

Above The tail of a Boeing 737 of Air Madagascar, the airline of the Malagasy Republic.
Left The insignia of Air Jamaica on the tail of a DC-8, the aircraft which operates the airline's long distance services.
Opposite top right The insignia of Air Malawi.
Opposite top left The insignia of the recently founded Air Malta.
Right A Boeing 720 of Air Malta. The code AP-AMJ on the rear fuselage reveals that the aircraft has been leased from Pakistan International, which has a substantial holding in Air Malta. In 1975 the 720 was the only aircraft in operation with Air Malta, used mainly for holiday traffic to Europe and three destinations, Manchester, Birmingham and Heathrow, in England.

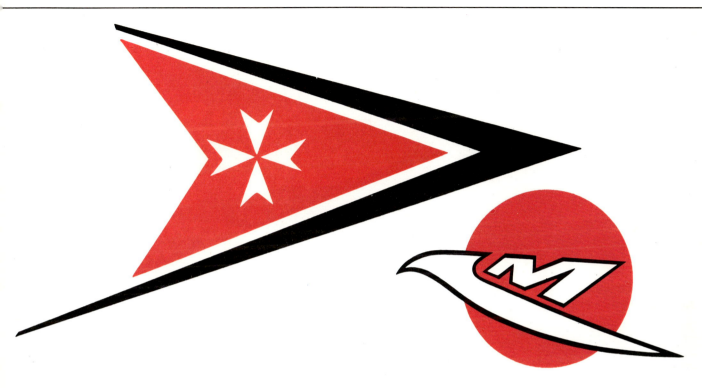

Air Malta

Head office: Luqa Airport, Malta.
Founded: 1973, with a five-year technical and management assistance programme with Pakistan International Airlines (which has 29 per cent shareholding).
Routes: Independent scheduled operations began in 1974, with a service to London, extending later to Birmingham and Manchester. Other routes planned in the near future include Rome, Tripoli, Frankfurt, Paris and Copenhagen.
Aircraft operated: Boeing 720.

Air Malawi

Head office: PO Box 84, Chileka International Airport, Blantyre, Malawi.
Founded: 1964, as a wholly-owned subsidiary of Central African Airways (CAA). Air Malawi became an independent company in 1967 following CAA's dissolution.
Routes: Domestic services from Blantyre to Karonga, Mzuzu, Lilongwe and Zomba. Regional services to Beira, Johannesburg, Lusaka, Ndola, Salisbury, Nairobi and the Seychelles. International services to London.
Aircraft operated: VC10; BAC 1-11; HS748; Viscount; Islander.

Air New Zealand

Head office: Air New Zealand House, 1 Queen Street, Auckland, New Zealand.

Founded: 1940, as Tasman Empire Airways. Name changed to Air New Zealand in 1965.

Routes: International services link Auckland, Wellington and Christchurch with Papeete, Honolulu, Los Angeles, Hong Kong, Singapore, Melbourne, Sydney, Brisbane, Norfolk Island, Noumea, Nandi and Pago Pago. Services to London started in 1975. Also DC-8 services operate to Raratonga in the Cook Islands. Air New Zealand has an interest in Cook Islands Airways, formed 1973 to provide an inter-island link between Raratonga and Aitutaki.

Aircraft operated: Douglas DC-8, DC-10.

Below The striking colour scheme of Air New Zealand's DC-10s. The airline uses its six models on the Auckland—Fiji—Honolulu—Los Angeles route, due to be extended to London in 1975 and thus bringing Air New Zealand colours (though British Airways will technically operate the service) to Heathrow for the first time. The symbol on the tail is a traditional Maori 'koru' emblem.

Left Sunset over Rainmaker Mountain from Pago Pago Airport in the Pacific islands of American Samoa. To the left of the cockpit of the DC-10 is the traditional Air New Zealand symbol, a flying fish.

Air Pacific
Air Rhodesia
Air Siam

Air Pacific

Head office: CML Buildings, Victoria Parade, Suva, Fiji.
Founded: 1951, as Fiji Airways, by Harold Gatty, the pioneer round-the-world airman. Name changed to Air Pacific in 1971.
Routes: Local services operate within the Fiji group of islands, and an internal service in the Gilbert and Ellice Islands. Regional services link Fiji with the New Hebrides, the Solomon Islands, Port Moresby, Tonga, Western Samoa, Nauru and Brisbane. Authority is now sought to extend operations to New Zealand, American Samoa, and the Marshall Islands.
Aircraft operated: BAC 1-11; HS748; Heron; Britten-Norman Trislander.

Air Rhodesia

Head office: PO Box AP1, Salisbury Airport, Salisbury, Rhodesia.
Founded: 1967, succeeding the Rhodesia element of the Central African Airways Corporation, dissolved in 1967.
Routes: Domestic network in operation. International services from Salisbury, Victoria Falls and Bulawayo to Johannesburg, and from Salisbury to Durban, Blantyre, Beira, Vilanculos and Lourenco Marques.
Aircraft operated: Boeing 720; Viscount 700; Douglas DC-3.

Air Siam

Head Office: 1643/5 New Petchburi Road, Bangkok, Thailand.
Founded: 1965.
Routes: International service from Bangkok to Hong Kong, Tokyo and Honolulu. Future plans envisage services to Singapore, Australia and the South Pacific, and to Europe.
Aircraft operated: Boeing 707, 747; Airbus 300B; Douglas DC-10.

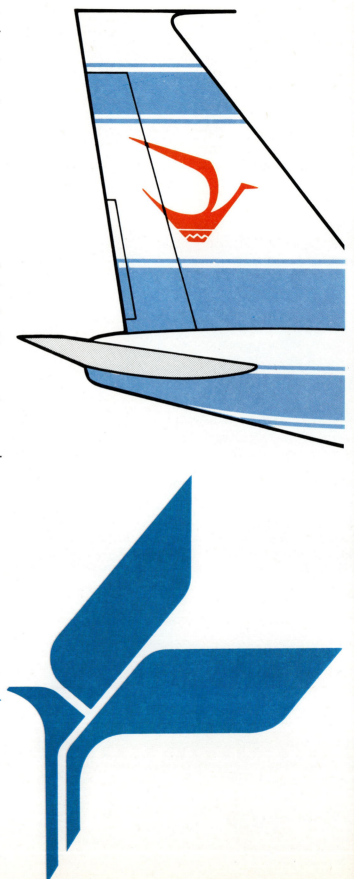

Left top The tail of a Boeing 720 of Air Rhodesia, used on the Salisbury—South Africa services of that airline.
Far left The shark-like symbol of Air Pacific, formerly called Fiji Airways.
Above The symbol remains the same but the name (to Air Pacific) and number (to DQ-FBH) have since changed with the airline's nominal expansion from 'Fiji' to the whole 'Pacific'. The Hawker Siddeley 748 is one of three in service with the airline in 1975.
Near left The insignia of Air Siam.
Right The dragon of Air Vietnam.

Air Vietnam

Head office: 27B Phan-dinh-Phung, Saigon, South Vietnam.
Founded: 1951, to take over the regional, international and domestic services previously operated by Air France.
Routes: Domestic services linking Saigon with principal towns. Regional and international services to Laos, Khmer (Cambodia), Formosa, Japan, Philippine Islands, Singapore, Malaysia, Hong Kong and Thailand.
Aircraft operated: Boeing 707, 727; Douglas DC-6 DC-4, DC-3; Cessna 185, Cessna 206.

Air Zaire

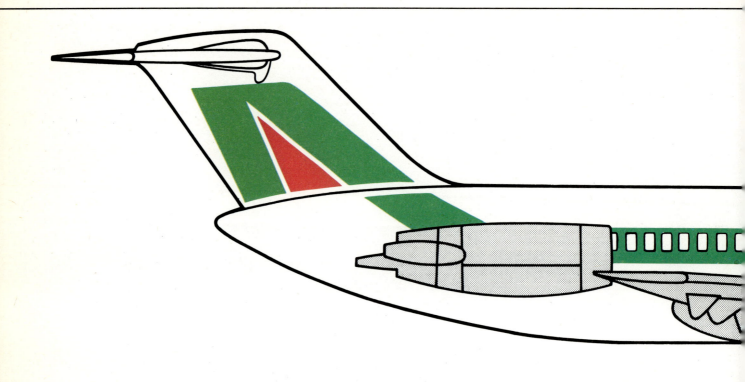

Air Zaire

Head office: 4 Avenue du Port, Kinshasa, Republic of Zaire.
Founded: 1961, as Air Congo. Name changed to Air Zaire in 1971.
Routes: Extensive domestic network operating from Kinshasa and Lubumbashi. International services to Abidjan, Athens, Bangui, Brussels, Bujumbura, Conakry, Dakar, Dar-es-Salaam, Donala, Entebbe, Frankfurt, Geneva, Libreville, Lome, Madrid, Nairobi, Ndjamena, Paris and Rome.
Aircraft operated: Boeing 747, 737; Douglas DC-10, DC-8, DC-4; Caravelle; Fokker F.27.

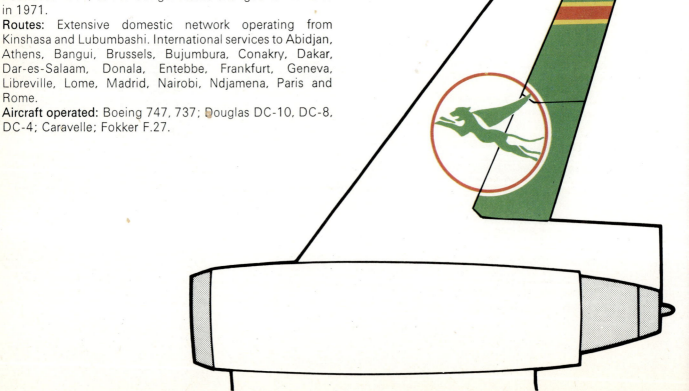

Alitalia

Head office: Palazzo Alitalia, Piazzale dell'Arte, Rome ER 00144, Italy.
Founded: 1946.
Routes: International services to other European countries, Africa, North and South America, the Middle and Far East and Australia. A domestic network between principal Italian cities is operated although a proportion of this traffic is diverted to Alitalia's subsidiary—Aerotrasporti Italiani (ATI). Another subsidiary, Societa Aerea Mediterranea (SAM) provides charter and inclusive-tour services. Alitalia also has a substantial interest in Somali Airlines.
Aircraft operated: Boeing 747; Douglas DC-10, DC-9, DC-8; Caravelle.

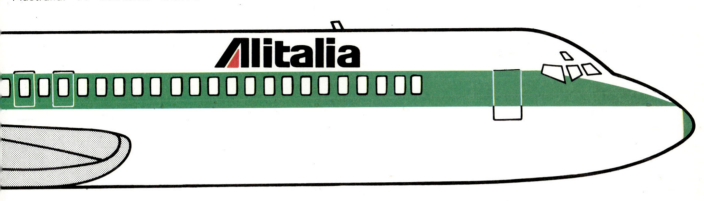

Alia Royal Jordanian Airlines

Head office: Insurance Building, First Circle, Jebel, Amman, Jordan.
Founded: 1963.
Routes: With emphasis on the tourist market, services are operated from Amman to Aqaba, Beirut, Cairo, Dubai, Muscat, Istanbul, Rabat, Nicosia, Jeddah, Dhahran, Kuwait, Doha, Abu Dhabi, Teheran, Karachi, Athens, Rome, Paris, Frankfurt, Madrid, London and Copenhagen.
Aircraft operated: Boeing 707, 720, 727; Caravelle.

Top A DC-9 of Alitalia, used by the Italian national airline on its European routes. Red green and white are the national colours.
Bottom left The tail of an Air Zaire DC-10. The symbol on the tail represents a leopard.
Bottom right The tail of a Boeing 720, used by Alia for its long range European routes.
Overleaf The first Air Zaire DC-10, 'Mont Ngaliema'. Rather than standardize operations, Air Zaire also leased the flagship of the Pan Am 747 fleet ('America', appropriately numbered N747PA) to share its European services, which terminate at Brussels.

All Nippon Airways (ANA)

Head office: Kasumigaseki Building, 3-2-5 Kasumigaseki, Tokyo, Japan.
Founded: 1958.
Routes: Domestic services to 35 main cities and towns. Regional charter services to nine points in Asia.
Aircraft operated: TriStar; Boeing 727, 737; YS-11A; Fokker F.27; Navajo; Sikorsky S-61N; Kawasaki KH-4.

American Airlines

Head office: 633 Third Avenue, New York 10017, USA.
Founded: 1934, to succeed American Airways and numerous earlier companies formed from 1926. In 1971 Trans Caribbean Airways was taken over and merged into the company. One of the world's largest airlines, (in the USA only United, Eastern and Delta carry more passengers), it has sponsored many important designs including the DC-3, CV-240, Electra and DC-10.
Routes: Extensive transcontinental network linking major US cities and towns, plus services, north, to Toronto, south, to Mexico City and Acapulco, and to Hawaii, Puerto Rico, the US Virgin Islands, Aruba, Curacao and Haiti. Non-transportation activities, including hotels, gift shops etc. are organized by Flagship International Inc.
Aircraft operated: Boeing 707, 727, 747; Douglas DC-10.

Below Perhaps the most attractive of all airline liveries is American's distinctive raw metallic, shown here on a Douglas DC-10, an airliner originally designed with American's requirements in mind. Though once operating as far afield as Europe and Australia, American have cut back their overseas routes in recent years and now operate solely within North America and the Caribbean.
Right The tail of a 727 of Japan's All Nippon Airways. The strange symbol on the tail is an early design suggested by Leonardo da Vinci for a helicopter.

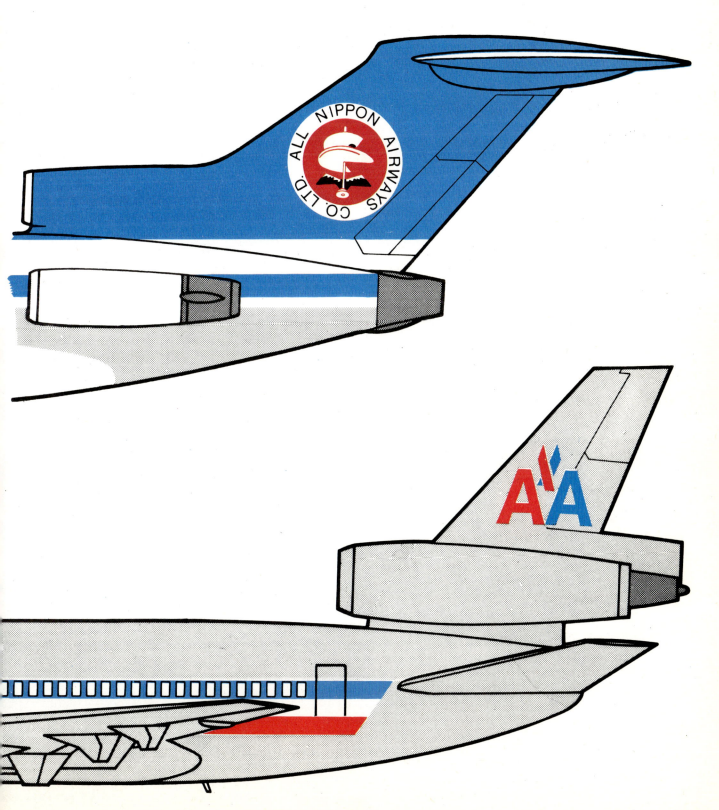

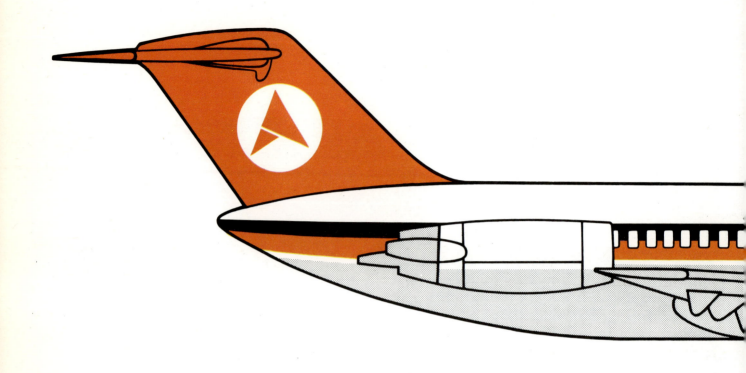

Above A DC-9 of
Australia's private airline
Ansett. All of the
subsidiary companies
carry the same livery but
some have different
lettering (for instance
MacRobertson-Miller in
Western Australia still
carry the letters MMA
rather than Ansett).
Below Another DC-9,
this time of Austrian
Airlines and used on its
European routes.

Ansett Airlines of Australia

Head office: 489 Swanston Street, Melbourne, Victoria, Australia.
Founded: 1936, as Ansett Airways. Since 1952 the company has successfully acquired control and taken over several regional and domestic airlines, becoming, in 1957, Australia's largest privately-owned airline. The airline interests are controlled by Ansett Transport Industries Inc, which includes Ansett Airlines of Australia; Ansett Airlines of South Australia; Ansett Airlines of New South Wales; and MacRobertson-Miller Airlines. In 1973, some aircraft and all routes of Ansett Airlines of Papua, New Guinea, passed to Air Niugini (airline of the newly-independent Republic of Niugini), though Ansett retained a 16 per cent shareholding.
Routes: Virtually dominating domestic air transport with TAA, an extensive network covers all of Australia's states, Lord Howe Island, and Papua and New Guinea. Helicopter services operate between the Yarra Heliport and Tulla-

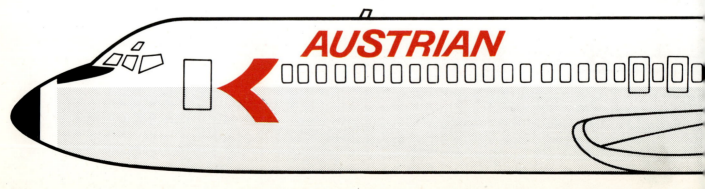

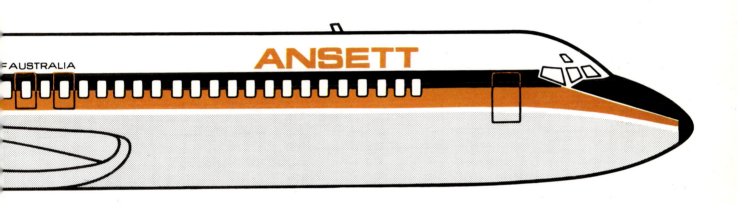

marine (Melbourne) and in the Barrier Reef, North Queensland.

Aircraft operated: Boeing 727; Douglas DC-9, DC-4; Fokker F.27, F.28; Electra freighter; Carvair; Twin Otter; Sikorsky S-61N and JetRanger.

Austrian Airlines-AUA (Oesterreichische Luftverkehrs)

Head office: A-1031 Vienna, Salesianergasse 1, Austria.
Founded: 1957.
Routes: International services from Vienna, Graz, Linz, Klagenfurt and Salzburg to major points in West Germany, Switzerland, Scandinavia, France, UK, Italy, Netherlands, Rumania, Yugoslavia, Greece, Bulgaria, Turkey, Lebanon, Israel, Poland, Hungary, Czechoslovakia, East Germany and USSR. Austrian Airtransport is a subsidiary company.
Aircraft operated: Douglas DC-9.

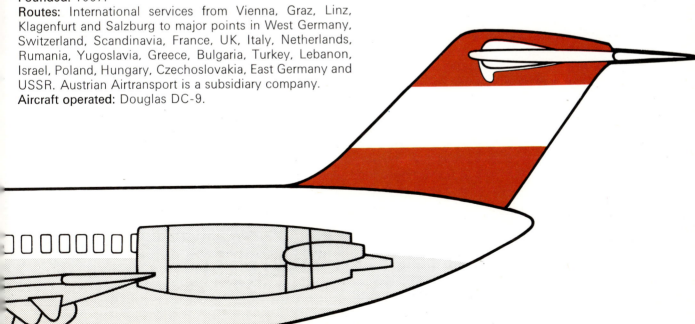

Avianca (Aerovias Nacionales de Colombia)
Bangladesh Biman (National Airlines of Bangladesh)

Avianca (Aerovias Nacionales de Colombia)

Head office: Carrera 7a, No 16–84, Bogota, Colombia.
Founded: 1940 as Avianca, following the merger of Sociedad Colombo-Alemana de Transportes Aereos (SCADTA) and Servicio Aereo Colombiano (SACO). Regarded as the oldest airline in the Americas as SCADTA had been established in 1919 by Colombian-German interests.
Routes: As the largest airline in South America Avianca has an extensive domestic network from Bogota, plus international services to Madrid, Paris, Frankfurt, Zurich, Miami, New York, Los Angeles, Panama, Mexico, Quito, Lima, Santiago and Buenos Aires.
Aircraft operated: Boeing 707, 720, 727; HS748; Douglas DC-3, DC-4.

Bangladesh Biman (National Airlines of Bangladesh)

Head office: Islam Chamber, 125A Motijheel Commercial Area, Dacca, Bangladesh.
Founded: 1972.
Routes: Services from Dacca to Chittagong, Sylhet, Jessore, Ishurdi, Comilla, Thakurgaon, Calcutta, Bangkok, Kathmandu and London.
Aircraft operated: Boeing 707 and Fokker F.27.

Left above The tail of a Boeing 707 belonging to Avianca, the Colombian airline which describes itself as 'the oldest in the Western Hemisphere', a claim disputed by KLM.
Left bottom The airline of newly-independent Bangladesh was founded with two 707s, the tails of which introduced this new colour scheme to the Dacca—London Heathrow route.
Far right The tail insignia of British Air Ferries, most commonly seen on their Carvairs which are DC-4s converted for vehicle-carrying services.
Near right The insignia of Braniff Airways, unique among the world's major airlines in having no single colour scheme.
Above right The symbol of the Thomson Organization's charter airline, the familiar figure of Britannia.
Overleaf One of the 14 Boeing 737s in operation with Britannia in 1975. Purchased new, they formed the complete fleet of an airline which became, with the demise of Court Line in 1974, the United Kingdom's largest wholly non-scheduled carrier. In the same year Britannia received permission to begin the first 'feeder' charter services—carrying passengers from Glasgow to Luton where they join their holiday flights.

Britannia Airways

Head office: Luton Airport, Luton, Bedfordshire, England.
Founded: 1961, as Euravia (London). In 1965 the airline was wholly taken over by the Thomson Organization. Luton Aircraft Engineers is a subsidiary.
Routes: Passenger and cargo charters and inclusive-tour services operated.
Aircraft operated: Boeing 737.

British Air Ferries (BAF)

Head office: Southend Airport, Southend-on-Sea, Essex, England.
Founded: 1962, as British United Air Ferries, following the merger of Channel Air Bridge (founded 1954 as Air Charter) and Silver City Airways (founded 1946 and pioneering cross-Channel vehicle air ferry services in 1948). Name changed to British Air Ferries in 1967. Ownership of the company was taken over from Air Holdings Limited by Transmeridian Air Cargo of Stansted in 1971.
Routes: Passenger, cargo and vehicle ferry services from Southend Airport to Le Touquet, Ostend, Rotterdam and Basle, with the Le Touquet and Ostend services linking with rail connections to Brussels, Amsterdam and Paris.
Aircraft operated: Carvair; Herald.

Braniff Airways

Head office: Exchange Park, Dallas, Texas 75235, USA.
Founded: Originally in 1928 as Braniff Air Lines, but was absorbed into Universal Aviation Corporation in 1929. The present airline was organized as an independent company in 1930.
Routes: Domestic services cover central US from Minneapolis/St Paul to Texas and Louisiana; extending eastwards to Tennessee, Washington DC and New York, from Texas to New Orleans, Tampa and Miami, and west to Denver, Seattle/Tacoma and Portland, and from five mainland cities in the south-east and south-west US to Hilo and Honolulu, Hawaii. South American services from Miami, New York, Washington DC, New Orleans, Houston, Los Angeles and San Francisco to Panama City, Bogota, Cali, Guayaquil, Quito, Lima, Sao Paulo, Rio de Janeiro, La Paz, Asuncion, Buenos Aires and Santiago. Services to Mexico City and Acapulco from the US operate via Dallas/Fort Worth, Houston and San Antonio. Braniff also operates MAC contract services.
Aircraft operated: Boeing 727, 747; Douglas DC-8.

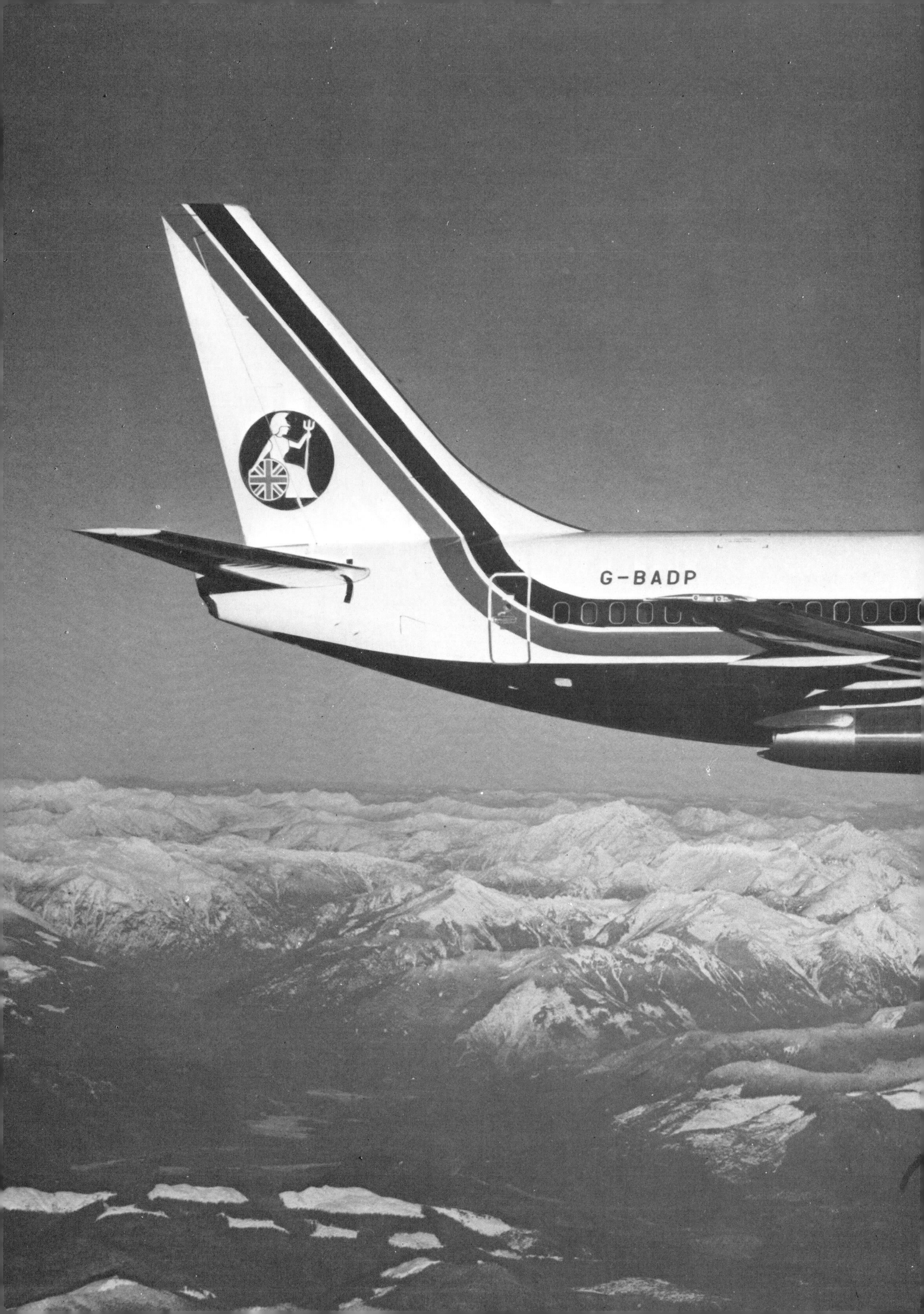
G-BADP

British Airways [The British Airways Board (BAB)]

Under the Civil Aviation Act of 1971, the British Airways Board was established to exercise control over the seven operating divisions which now form the British Airways Group. On April 1, 1975 the various national corporations within BAG were dissolved and the whole Group began trading as a single airline, known as BRITISH AIRWAYS. While coming only sixth in terms of the actual number of passengers carried, British Airways is almost certainly the world's largest transporter of international traffic, largely because of its intense European and trans-Atlantic network. It has the longest route mileage of any airline in the world,

employs more staff than any airline other than United, receives more in revenue, flies to more international destinations, and has the highest operating expenditure of any airline in the world.

Head office: Victoria Terminal, Buckingham Palace Road, London SW1.

The operating divisions of British Airways include:—

EUROPEAN DIVISION—formerly the British European Airways Corporation and BEA Division.

Head office: Bealine House, Ruislip, Middlesex, England.

Founded: 1946, as a state enterprise, to take over BOAC's European and domestic routes. The present Division com-

prises three components: the Super One-Eleven Division (based in Manchester), the Cargo Division, and British Airtours Limited, which operates charter and inclusive-tour services from Gatwick.

Routes: As the largest air traffic operator in Europe, scheduled passenger and cargo services cover all major European cities and several points in the Middle East. Most international services are operated in pool with other European carriers. Domestic services account for over a third of the European Division's operations.

Aircraft operated: Trident One, Two and Three; BAC 1-11; Vanguard; Merchantman; Boeing 707; TriStar.

OVERSEAS DIVISION—formerly the British Overseas Airways Corporation and BOAC Division.

Head office: Speedbird House, Heathrow Airport, Hounslow, Middlesex, England.

Founded: 1939, as a result of the government merger of Imperial Airways—founded in 1924, and having its origins in Britain's first commercial air transport company which began the world's first regularly scheduled international passenger service, between London and Paris, in 1919—and the original British Airways—founded in 1935. During the Second World War BOAC played a vital role in keeping open essential lines of air communications, also pioneering the North Atlantic Return Ferry Service, which was the first regular, year-round air service operating in both directions across the North Atlantic. In 1946, domestic and European services were transferred to the new BEA and routes to South America were given to British South American Airways Corporation, a second new airline, which was later merged with BOAC in 1949. The world's first commercial jet services were introduced by BOAC in 1952 with the Comet 1.

Routes: The Overseas Division operates the world's largest route network, linking the UK with major cities and points in every continent, and includes several round-the-world services. British Overseas Air Charter is currently part of the Overseas Division and operates charter and inclusive-tour services.

Aircraft operated: Boeing 707, 747; VC10; Concorde.

Far left A Boeing 707 of the British Airways charter subsidiary, British Airtours. Based at Gatwick, the subsidiary's seven 707s work almost entirely in the package holiday area.

Below A Boeing 747 of the Overseas Division of British Airways. The symbol below the flight deck is the old BOAC insignia, the 'Speedbird' and the design on the tail is a stylized version of the Union Jack. It is British Airways proud boast that it flies more route miles to more international destinations than any other airline in the world. The 747s are used mainly on the North Atlantic, Australian and South African routes, but may also be seen in Tokyo and the West Indies. The Overseas Division's predecessor, BOAC, was the first airline in the world to operate a commercial jet service and also the first to run a jet Trans-Atlantic schedule, though Aeroflot seemed likely to precede it in introducing the world's first supersonic passenger services.

BRITISH AIRWAYS REGIONAL DIVISION

Regional Division is composed of what was British Air Services (founded 1967 and operating as Northeast Airlines, Cambrian Airways) and the Scottish Airways and Channel Islands Airways Divisions of BEA. Each airline will probably retain its name as a means of regional identity.

Head office: Hodford House, 17–27 High Street, Hounslow, Middlesex.

Main regional office: Cardiff (Cambrian).

Bases: Leeds/Bradford (Northeast)
　　　　Glasgow (Scottish)
　　　　Jersey (Channel Islands)

Routes: Scheduled domestic passenger and cargo services. International services from the provinces to major Continental cities, with certain services to provincial European cities from London.

Aircraft operated: Trident One; BAC 1-11; Viscount; Skyliner; HS748.

BRITISH AIRWAYS HELICOPTERS — formerly BEA Helicopters Ltd.

Head office: Gatwick Airport South, Horley, Surrey, England.

Founded: 1964, to take over and develop BEA's helicopter activities which had begun on an experimental basis in 1948 with a summer mail service in East Anglia. In 1950 BEA initiated the world's first scheduled passenger helicopter service linking Cardiff with Liverpool via Wrexham. This service was discontinued the following year but further experimental operations were tried in various areas.

Routes: Scheduled services between Penzance and the Isles of Scilly. Contract work includes off-shore oil and gas rig support operations, primarily in the North Sea area, and search and rescue operations covering Scotland's northeast coast. Charter flights are also undertaken.

Aircraft operated: Sikorsky S-61N and S-58T; Bell 212; JetRanger.

BRITISH AIRWAYS ASSOCIATED COMPANIES—formerly BOAC Associated Companies.

Exercises control of the world-wide hotel and other travel-related undertakings of British Airways Group and of its investment activities in Air Mauritius, Air Pacific, Cathay Pacific Airways, Cyprus Airways, Gibraltar Airways, New Hebrides Airways and Turk Hava Yollari (THY Turkish Airlines).

Head office: Speedbird House, Heathrow Airport, Hounslow, Middlesex, England.

BRITISH AIRWAYS ENGINE OVERHAUL—formerly BOAC Engine Overhaul.

Responsible for engine overhauls for British Airways and several other airlines.

Head office: Treforest Industrial Estate, Pontypridd, Glamorgan, South Wales.

BRITISH AIRWAYS TRAVEL DIVISION

Founded 1973 to handle UK sales on behalf of the European, Overseas and Regional Divisions.

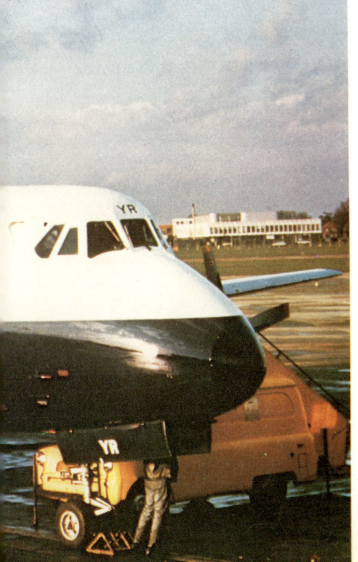

Left A BAC (Vickers) Viscount of the Regional Division of British Airways in the new British Airways colours. These aircraft formed the backbone of the Regional Division's fleet in the mid-1970s, operating the services of the Cambrian, Scottish, Channel Islands and, as in this example, Northeast sections. The Cambrian and Northeast subsidiaries both have their own IATA booking codes (CS and NS) and for several years used their own colour schemes (Cambrian in red and Northeast in yellow). The trend at present, however, is to paint the whole British Airways fleet (numbering some 220 aircraft in 1975) in the new colours. The Northeast Viscounts can most often be seen operating the Heathrow to Leeds/Bradford and Newcastle services but some venture further afield to Bordeaux and Luxembourg. The Regional Division mainly uses its planes on internal routes with a heavy emphasis on Channel Island services to both Jersey and Guernsey.
Opposite top At the other end of the British Airways fleet are the five Concordes due to go into service on the Overseas Division's routes in 1976.

This page Two of three scheduled airlines (the other is Dan-Air) which operate principally out of London's second airport, Gatwick, had their origins in British United Airways. British Caledonian remains the UK's second scheduled operator, having been given some of BOAC's South American and African routes. British Island Airways was 'left over' when Caledonian/BUA was formed in 1970. With a fleet of Heralds, BIA is easily the largest operator of this aircraft.
Above 'Isle of Bute', one of British Caledonian's BAC 1-11 short haul jets.
Below British Caledonian colours on a 707 used by the airline on all its intercontinental services and long-distance charters. The tail design represents the lion rampant of Scotland.
Right The insignia of British Island Airways.

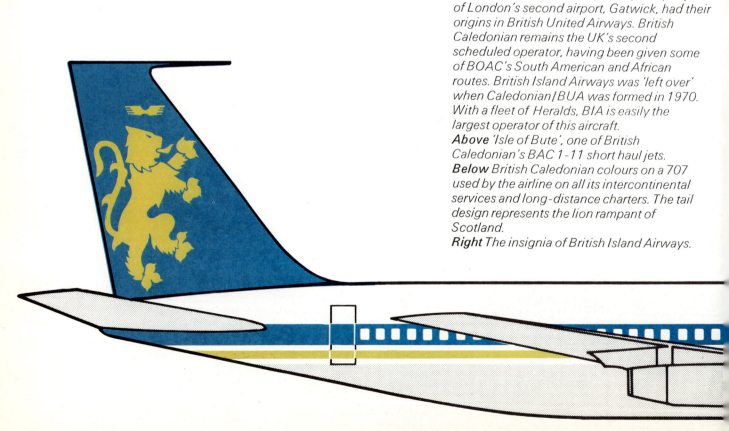

British Caledonian Airways (BCAL)

Head office: Gatwick Airport, Horley, Surrey, England.

Founded: 1970, as Caledonian/BUA, following the merger of two of Britain's leading independent airlines, Caledonian Airways (founded 1961) and British United Airways (formed in 1960 as a result of a merger). Name changed to British Caledonian Airways in 1971.

Routes: Domestic services from Gatwick to Belfast, Edinburgh, Glasgow, Jersey, Manchester, Newcastle and Southampton. Extensive network of scheduled European and intercontinental services (principally to Africa) operated from Gatwick, together with worldwide passenger and charter flights.

Aircraft operated: Boeing 707; BAC 1-11.

British Island Airways (BIA)

Head office: Berkeley House, 51-53 High Street, Redhill, Surrey, England.

Founded: 1968, as British United Islands Airways (BUIA) following a reconstitution of British United Airways group interests. The origins of the airline are, however, rooted in much earlier companies, principally Jersey Airlines, Morton Air Services and Manx Airlines. Name changed to British Island Airways in 1970—the year BUA, *but not* BUIA, was sold to Caledonian Airways.

Routes: Network of short-haul passenger and cargo services links London, the Channel Islands, the Isle of Man, Southampton, Exeter, Dublin, Belfast, Blackpool, Manchester, Glasgow, Edinburgh, Paris, Antwerp, Hanover and Dusseldorf. Ad hoc charter and contract operations also undertaken.

Aircraft operated: Herald.

British Midland Airways (BMA)
British West Indian Airways (BWIA International)

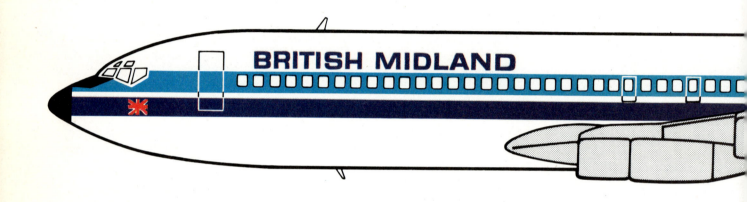

British Midland Airways (BMA)

Head office: East Midlands Airport, Castle Donington, Derby, England.

Founded: 1947, as Derby Airways. Name changed to British Midland Airways in 1964.

Routes: Scheduled services from the East Midlands to Paris, Glasgow, Belfast, Dublin, Amsterdam, Brussels, Frankfurt, Jersey and Guernsey (the last four via Birmingham); from London to Tees-side, Strasbourg, Aberdeen, Belfast and Newquay and from Southend to Jersey and Guernsey. Charter and inclusive-tour flights also undertaken. In addition, in 1972 BMA began operating international services for Sudan Airways.

Aircraft operated: Boeing 707; Herald; Viscount.

British West Indian Airways (BWIA International)

Head office: Sunjet House, 30 Edward Street, Port of Spain, Trinidad.

Founded: 1940. In 1947 the airline was acquired by British South American Airways which, in 1949, merged with BOAC. BWIA was therefore a subsidiary of BOAC up until 1961 when the Trinidad Government bought 90 percent of the stock and the remaining 10 percent in 1967.

Routes: Network of scheduled passenger and cargo services to points in the Caribbean area, and to New York, Toronto, Miami, Guyana and London.

Aircraft operated: Boeing 707.

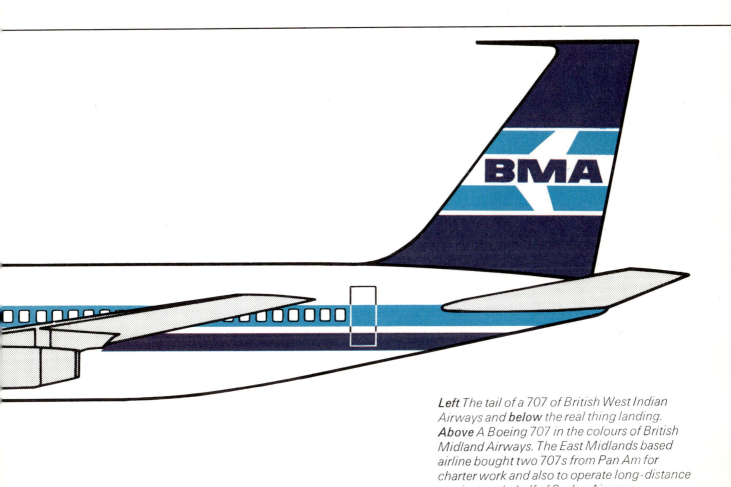

Left The tail of a 707 of British West Indian Airways and below the real thing landing. Above A Boeing 707 in the colours of British Midland Airways. The East Midlands based airline bought two 707s from Pan Am for charter work and also to operate long-distance services on behalf of Sudan Airways.

Cathay Pacific Airways
Ceskoslovenske Aerolinie (CSA)
China Airlines (CAL)

Top The insignia of Ceskoslovenske Aerolinie. The Czech airliners all carry the motif 'OK JET' on their tails.
Above A familiar sight on the Far Eastern and Pacific routes of Cathay Pacific are that airlines' 707s. The Union Jack on the tail indicates its being based in Hong Kong.
Opposite page The tail of a Boeing 727 of China Airlines, the Nationalist China airline based in Formosa (Taiwan).

Cathay Pacific Airways

Head office: Union House, 9 Connaught Road, Hong Kong.
Founded: 1946.
Routes: Scheduled passenger services from Hong Kong to Tokyo, Seoul, Osaka, Fuknoka, Taipei, Manila, Bangkok, Saigon, Kuala Lumpur, Kota, Kinabalu, Brunei, Singapore, Jakarta and Perth.
Aircraft operated: Boeing 707; TriStar.

China Airlines (CAL)

Head office: 26 Nanking Road East, 3rd Section, Taipei, Taiwan.
Founded: 1959.
Routes: Domestic services to all major cities within Taiwan (Nationalist China). Regional and international services from Taipei to Hong Kong, Tokyo, San Francisco, Seoul, Osaka, Okinawa, Bangkok, Manila, Saigon, Singapore, Kuala Lumpur, Honolulu, Los Angeles and Djakarta.
Aircraft operated: Boeing 707, 727; Caravelle III; YS-11A; Douglas DC-4, DC-3.

Ceskoslovenske Aerolinie (CSA)

Head office: Praha 6, Ruzyne Airport, Czechoslovakia.

Founded: 1945/6 by the government to reinstitute the civil air transport services which, before the Second World War, had been operated by Czechoslovak State Airlines (founded 1923) and the independent Ceskoslovenska Letecka Spolecnost (CLS) (founded 1927).

Routes: Extensive domestic network linking major towns and numerous small communities with trunkline cities. International services, operating within one of Europe's most intensive networks, to most European capitals, the Near, Middle and Far East, North and West Africa, and North and Central America. CSA also provides crop dusting, forestry patrol and other non-transport services.

Aircraft operated: Ilyushin Il-62, Il-14; Tupolev Tu-134A.

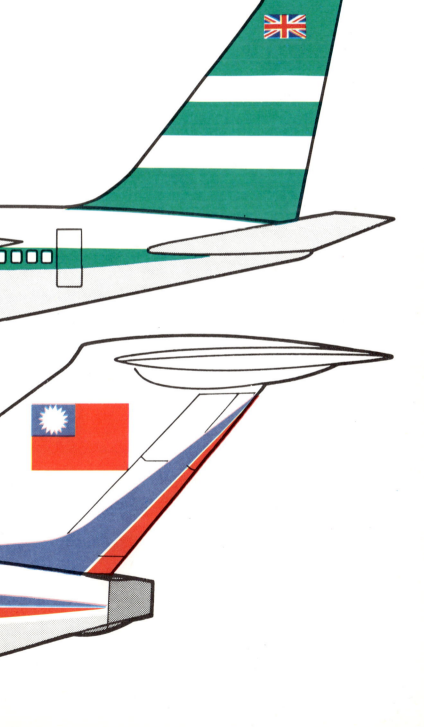

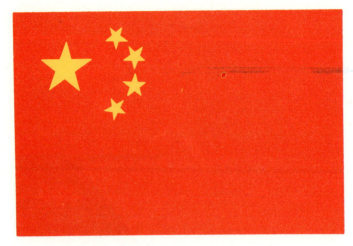

Civil Aviation Administration of China (CAAC)

Head office: 15 Chang An Street East, Peking, Peoples Republic of China.

Founded: 1954, following the Chinese acquisition of Aeroflot's half interest in the joint Soviet-Chinese airline, Skoga, and the merging of all existing civil air undertakings into a single operation. The airline operates within the jurisdiction of the General Bureau of Civil Aviation, an agency which is responsible for all non-military aviation activities; CAAC's operations extend to aerial survey, emergency, agricultural and forestry and other duties.

Routes: Domestic services linking Peking and provincial centres. International services between Peking-Irkutsk, Peking-Shenyang-Pyongyang, Kunming-Rangoon, Canton-Hanoi, and to Tirana (Albania) via Teheran and Bucharest, and Moscow. Future routes could include points in Ethiopia, Canada, Zaire, Iraq, and Algeria, and Karachi, Colombo, Belgrade, Paris, Dar-es-Salaam.

Aircraft operated: CAAC has ordered several modern jet-airliners from the west, thereby lessening Chinese reliance on Soviet equipment and spares. Current types are: Boeing 707; Trident One, Two and Three; Viscount 800; Ilyushin Il-62, Il-18, Il-14, Il-12; Antonov An-12, An-24, An-2, An-14; Lisunov Li-2; Super Aero 45; Mil Mi-2.

Above The flag of the Chinese People's Republic, carried on the tail of the aircraft in their varied fleet.
Opposite top The tail of a Continental DC-10.
Below The dramatic lines of a CP Air 747. Canada's second airline uses these aircraft mainly on its routes from Vancouver to Honolulu and Tokyo on to Hong Kong.

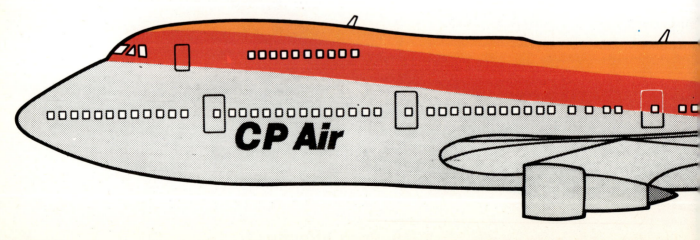

Continental Air Lines

Head office: Los Angeles International Airport, California, USA.

Founded: 1934, as Varney Speed Lines, becoming Varney Air Transport five months later. Name changed to Continental Air Lines in 1937.

Routes: Services linking south west regions of the US with the Pacific north west; routes from Houston to Los Angeles, via San Antonio, El Paso, Tucson and Phoenix; from Chicago to Los Angeles via Kansas City and Denver, and from Los Angeles to Hawaii which may be extended to Sydney.

Aircraft operated: Boeing 747, 720, 727; Douglas DC-10, DC-9, DC-6.

CP Air

Head office: Granville Square, Vancouver, BC, Canada.

Founded: 1942, as Canadian Pacific Airlines Ltd. by Canadian Pacific Railway in an amalgamation of ten small airlines (bush operators). Name changed to CP Air in 1968.

Routes: Domestic trunk services from Vancouver, Calgary, Edmonton, Winnipeg, Toronto, Ottawa and Montreal. International services to Hong Kong, Tokyo, Sydney, Fiji, Honolulu, San Francisco, Mexico City, Guadalajara, Puerta Vallarta, Acapulco, Lima, Santiago, Buenos Aires, Tel-Aviv, Lisbon, Madrid, Rome, Milan, Athens and Amsterdam.

Aircraft operated: Boeing 747, 727, 737; Douglas DC-8.

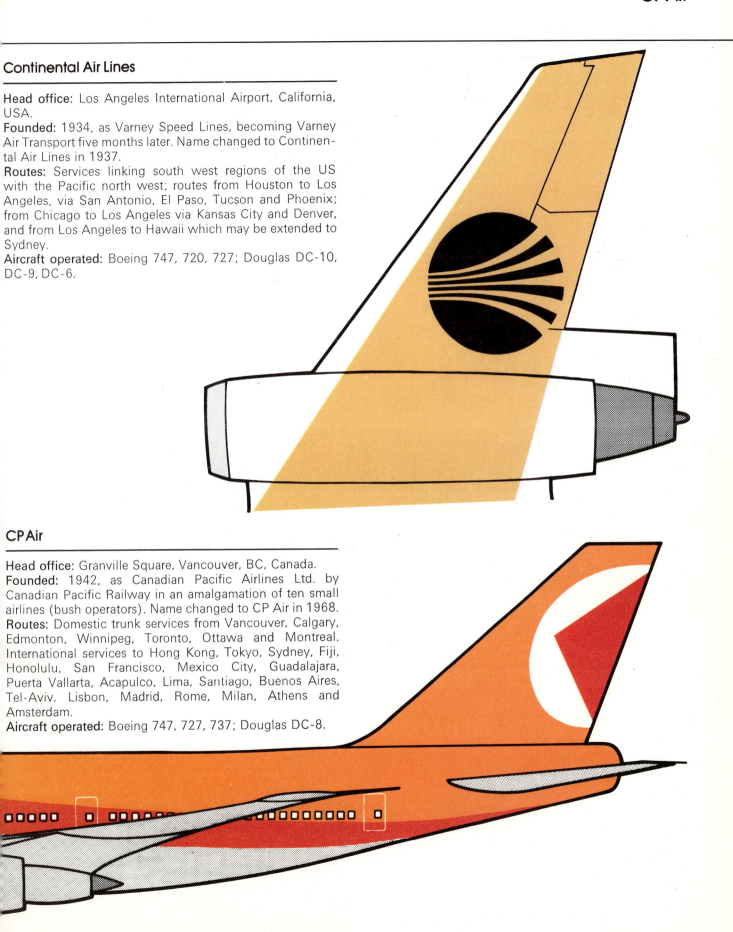

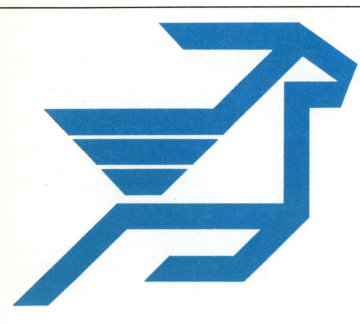

Dan-Air Services

Head office: Bilbao House, 36-38 New Broad Street, London EC2, England.
Founded: 1953, originally for charter work, but recent years have seen the growth of an extensive programme of inclusive-tour flights under contract to several major tour operators DAN-AIR INTERCONTINENTAL (founded 1970) is a subsidiary specializing in trans-Atlantic charter operations. Skyways International was acquired in 1972.
Routes: Extensive domestic network linking Newcastle, Manchester, Bristol, Cardiff, Liverpool, Carlisle, Leeds, Glasgow, Birmingham, Bournemouth, Gatwick and Luton. International services from Gatwick to Berne, Ostend, Clermont Ferrand and Montpellier; from Bristol, Liverpool and Tees-side to Amsterdam; from Newcastle to Kristiansand and Stavanger; and from Ashford to Beauvais. Services to the Channel Islands are operated from Ashford, Gatwick, Bournemouth and Swansea.
Aircraft operated: Boeing 727, 707; Comet; BAC 1-11; HS748.

Cyprus Airways

Head office: 21 Athanassiou Dhiakou Street, Nicosia, Cyprus.
Founded: 1947.
Routes: Services from Nicosia to Beirut, Tel-Aviv, Cairo, Brussels, Ankara, Istanbul, Athens, Rome, Frankfurt, London and Manchester.
Aircraft operated: Trident One and Two.

Delta Air Lines

Head office: Hartsfield Atlanta International Airport, Atlanta, Georgia 30320, USA.
Founded: 1925, as the world's first crop-spraying operation; passenger services began in 1929. Delta is the third largest American airline (and thus fourth in the world) carrying nearly 25 million passengers in 1973.
Routes: Nationwide services linking major cities and towns in the US. International services to Canada, Bermuda, the Bahamas, Caribbean and South America.
Aircraft operated: Boeing 747, 727; Douglas DC-10, DC-9, DC-8; TriStar; Fokker (Fairchild) F.27.

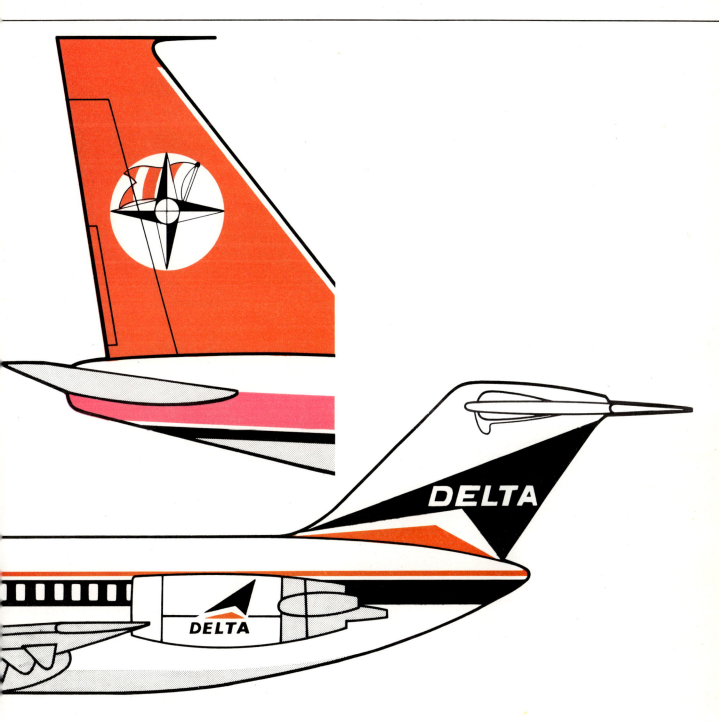

Top left The insignia of Cyprus Airways. The future of the airline was thrown into doubt with the Greco-Turkish clashes of 1974. The airline's home base, Nicosia Airport, remained closed after the fighting and both communities decided to build their own airport. As a result it seemed likely that two new airlines would come into being in 1975, though the Greek community may retain the old name.
This page top The compass insignia of Dan-Air on the tail of a Boeing 707, used by the airline for long-distance, mainly trans-Atlantic, charters. Dan-Air should not be confused with Danair, the Danish scheduled operator which has a series of domestic routes within Denmark.
Above A DC-9 of Delta Air Lines of Atlanta.

Previous pages The longer range member of Delta's Douglas fleet, the DC-8, used largely on the Florida—New York/Boston services. Delta also have slanting rather than vertical lettering on some planes.

East African Airways (EAA)
Eastern Air Lines
East-West Airlines

Above *The Lion of East Africa, symbol of East African Airways.*
Below right *The insignia of Australia's independent carrier, East-West Airlines.*

East African Airways (EAA)

Head office: Sadler House, Koinange Street, Nairobi, Kenya.
Founded: 1946, to provide air transport within and between the joint participants in the company, Kenya, Uganda, and Tanganyika—now Tanzania.
Routes: Extensive network of domestic services to all three countries from Nairobi, Mombasa, Dar-es-Salaam, Arusha and Entebbe. International services to Aden, Addis Ababa, Athens, Blantyre, Bombay, Bujumbura, Copenhagen, Frankfurt, Karachi, Kigali, London, Lusaka, Mauritius, Mogadishu, Zurich, Rome and Tananarive. In addition, passenger and cargo charter services are operated by a subsidiary company, Simbair known formerly as Seychelles-Kilimanjaro Air Transport (SKAT).
Aircraft operated: Super VC10; Boeing 747; Douglas DC-9, DC-3; Fokker F.27.

Eastern Air Lines

Head office: 10 Rockefeller Plaza, New York, NY10020, USA.
Founded: Originally in 1926 as Pitcairn Aviation, and taken over by North American Aviation in 1929. In 1938, the company was reorganized on an independent basis and its present name, Eastern Air Lines, adopted. Eastern is the second largest American airline to United and carried over 26 million passengers in 1973.
Routes: Domestic services to more than 100 cities in 30 states in the USA and the District of Columbia, with an Air-Shuttle service operated between Boston, Washington and New York. International services to Canada, Mexico, Puerto Rico, the Bahamas, Jamaica, the Virgin Islands and Bermuda.
Aircraft operated: TriStar; Douglas DC-9, DC-8; Boeing 727; Electra.

East-West Airlines

Head office: PO Box 249, Tamworth 2340, New South Wales, Australia.
Founded: 1947.
Routes: Formed purely as a domestic operation, EWA provides services to 29 centres in New South Wales, Queensland, Victoria, and Northern Territory. Charter flights are also undertaken, together with the operation of Twin Otter, DC-3 and Queen Air aircraft for the CSIRO and NSW Air Ambulance organizations. In addition, East-West has acquired the Adastra group of companies, involved in aerial survey and exploration work.
Aircraft operated: Fokker F.27.

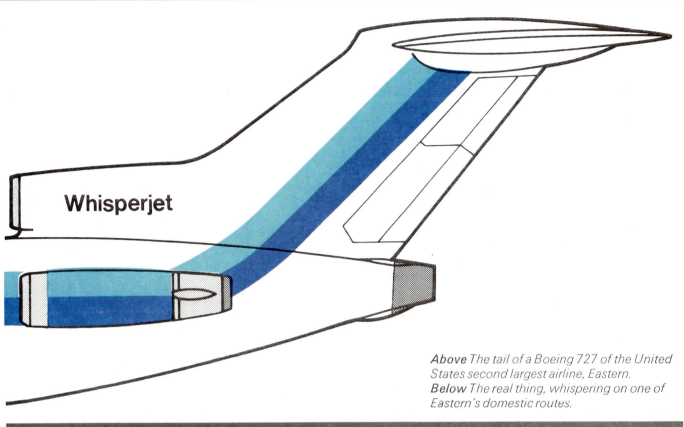

Whisperjet

Above The tail of a Boeing 727 of the United States second largest airline, Eastern.
Below The real thing, whispering on one of Eastern's domestic routes.

EgyptAir

Head office: Cairo International Airport, Arab Republic of Egypt.
Founded: 1932, as Misr Airwork; became United Arab Airlines from 1960 until 1971, when the present name EgyptAir was adopted.
Routes: Domestic services operated. International services to points in the Middle East, Africa, Eastern and Western Europe, and to Bombay, Bangkok, Hong Kong, Manila and Tokyo.
Aircraft operated: Boeing 707; Comet 4C; Antonov An-24.

Left The tail of a Boeing 707, used by EgyptAir on the majority of its long distance services.

Above Line up at Ben Gurion International Airport (formerly Lod), Tel Aviv, showing the difference in size between the El Al 747 and its smaller brothers, the 707 and 720.
Below A 747 of El Al, Israel's national airline. Note the Star of David on the tail.

El Al Israel Airlines

Head office: PO Box 41, Ben Gurion Airport, Israel.
Founded: 1948.
Routes: Regional services to Teheran, Istanbul and Cyprus. International services operate within three principal route patterns, i.e. North Atlantic between New York and European gateways; Tel-Aviv to most European capitals, and the African routes linking Tel-Aviv to Nairobi, Addis Ababa and Johannesburg. Direct services link Tel-Aviv/New York and Tel-Aviv/Montreal. El Al also has an interest in Arkia, Israel's domestic airline.
Aircraft operated: Boeing 747, 707 and 720.

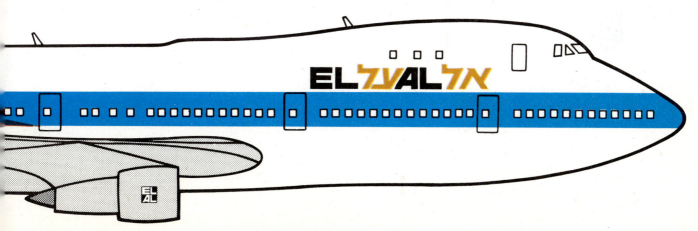

Ethiopian Airlines
Finnair

Ethiopian Airlines

Head office: PO Box 1755, International Airport, Addis Ababa, Ethiopia.
Founded: 1945.
Routes: Extensive domestic network linking many otherwise remote centres. International services to points in Africa, Europe, the Middle East, India and Pakistan.
Aircraft operated: Boeing 707 and 720.

Finnair

Head office: Mannerheimintie 102, Helsinki 25, Finland.
Founded: 1924, as Aero Oy. One of the world's oldest airlines, it operated exclusively with seaplanes until Finland's first airports were opened in 1936. In 1956 it became the first Western European airline to serve Moscow. Name changed to Finnair in 1968.
Routes: Domestic services to 18 points in Finland. Regional services from Helsinki to 20 principal European cities including Moscow and Leningrad. International service to New York.
Aircraft operated: Douglas DC-10, DC-9, DC-8; Super Caravelle; Convair CV-440; Beech Debonair.

The Flying Tiger Line

Head office: 7401 World Way West, Los Angeles International Airport, Los Angeles, California 90009, USA.

Founded: 1945, as National Skyway Freight Corporation, being the first *all-cargo* airline in the USA. Name changed to The Flying Tiger Line in 1946 after a famous wartime section of the United States Air Force.

Routes: Scheduled coast-to-coast cargo services within the USA. International scheduled cargo services to Tokyo, Hong Kong, Taipei, Osaka, Okinawa, Seoul, Manila, Bangkok and Saigon. Authority to operate services to Singapore, Kuala Lumpur and Djakarta was being sought in 1974. World-wide freight charters are also undertaken as well as trans-Pacific contract operations for MAC.

Aircraft operated: Douglas DC-8; Boeing 747.

Opposite top The East African Lion insignia of Ethiopian Airlines.
Left The symbol of Finnair.
Below left A Finnair DC-9, used on the airline's European services.
Below The tail of a DC-8 of The Flying Tiger Line, America's all-cargo carrier.
Overleaf A Flying Tiger 747 freighter.

Garuda Indonesian Airways

Head office: Djalan Ir H Djuanda 15, Djakarta, Indonesia.
Founded: 1950, by the government and KLM in succession to KLM's pre-war-island division.
Routes: Domestic and internationally from Djakarta to Hong Kong, Sydney, South East Asia and Europe terminating in Amsterdam.
Aircraft operated: Fokker F.27, F.28; Douglas DC-8, DC-9, DC-10; Convair CV-340.

Ghana Airways

Head office: PO Box 1636, Ghana House, Accra, Ghana.
Founded: 1958.
Routes: Domestic services from Accra to Takoradi, Kumasi and Tamale. Regional services to Abidjan, Monrovia, Freetown, Bangui and Dakar. International services from Accra to Lagos, Beirut, London and Rome.
Aircraft operated: VC10; Fokker F.28; Viscount; HS748; Douglas DC-3.

Below The insignia carried on the tail of all Garuda planes.
The national airline was founded after Indonesian independence from the Netherlands but Garuda still retains close links with KLM.
Bottom The insignia of Ghana Airways.

Gulf Air

Head office: PO Box 138, Bahrain.
Founded: 1950, by the governments of Bahrain, Qatar, Abu Dhabi and Oman. British Airways held 24 percent until 1974.
Routes: The basic trunk route is London-Beirut-Bahrain-Bombay. There is a service of local routes around the Persian Gulf based on Bahrain and Dubai.
Aircraft operated: VC-10; BAC 1-11; Fokker F.27.

Hughes Airwest

Head office: San Francisco International Airport, San Francisco, California 94128, USA.
Founded: 1968, as Air West. Present form of the name adopted in 1971.
Routes: Passenger and cargo services to 74 points in the west of the USA, to Calgary in Canada and to Guadalajara, Guaymas, Puerto Vallarta, La Paz and Mazatlan in Mexico.
Aircraft operated: Douglas DC-9; Fokker (Fairchild) F.27.

Below The arabic script for Gulf Air, carried prominently on the side of the airline's fleet. Gulf Air's VC-10s can be seen as far afield as London and Bombay.
Bottom Another stylish form of lettering which also acts as an insignia, that of Hughes Airwest.

Iberia (Lineas Aereas de Espana)
Icelandair (Flugfelag Islands HF) and Loftleidir (Icelandic Airlines)

Iberia (Lineas Aereas de Espana)

Head office: Valazquez 130, Madrid 6, Spain.
Founded: 1940, originally as a mainly domestic airline, with overseas services to Palma, Morocco and the Canary Islands.
Routes: Domestic services between principal cities and tourist centres. International services to major western European cities, to London, Manchester, Glasgow and Dublin, and to South and Central America, Africa and the USA, linking, in many instances, directly with tourist centres.
Aircraft operated: Boeing 747, 727; Douglas DC-10, DC-9, DC-8, DC-3; Caravelle; Fokker F.28, F.27; Airbus A300.

Icelandair (Flugfelag Islands HF) and Loftleidir (Icelandic Airlines)

Head offices: Icelandair: Baendahollin, Reykjavik, Iceland. Loftleidir: Reykjavik Airport, Iceland.
Founded: The two airline companies merged in 1973 under the holding company, Flugleidir, but will continue to operate independently and will retain their own names. Icelandair was founded in 1937 as Flugfelag Akureyrar; Loftleidir in 1944. International Air Bahama and Cargolux Airlines International (one-third holding) are both subsidiary companies of Loftleidir.
Routes: Icelandair: Domestic services linking Reykjavik to 12 centres. International services to Copenhagen, Oslo, Gothenburg, Frankfurt, Bergen, the Faroe Islands, Glasgow and London. Loftleidir: International services linking New York and Reykjavik to Glasgow, London, Luxembourg, Copenhagen, Stockholm and Oslo.
Aircraft operated: Boeing 727; Douglas DC-3, DC-8; Fokker F.27.

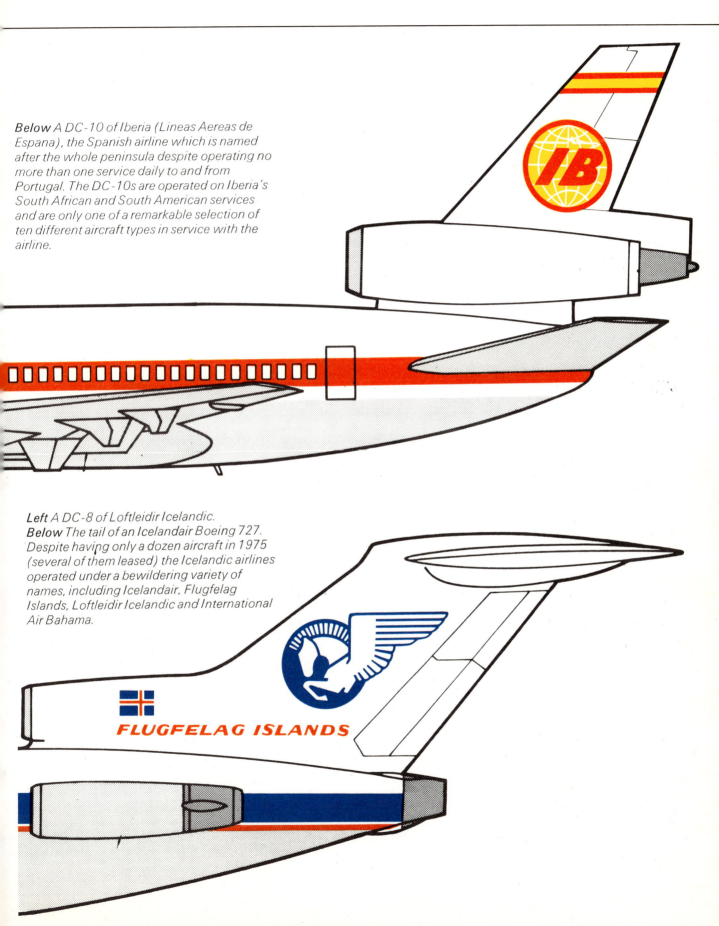

Below A DC-10 of Iberia (Lineas Aereas de Espana), the Spanish airline which is named after the whole peninsula despite operating no more than one service daily to and from Portugal. The DC-10s are operated on Iberia's South African and South American services and are only one of a remarkable selection of ten different aircraft types in service with the airline.

Left A DC-8 of Loftleidir Icelandic.
Below The tail of an Icelandair Boeing 727. Despite having only a dozen aircraft in 1975 (several of them leased) the Icelandic airlines operated under a bewildering variety of names, including Icelandair, Flugfelag Islands, Loftleidir Icelandic and International Air Bahama.

FLUGFELAG ISLANDS

Invicta International Airlines
Iran Air (Iran National Airlines Corporation)
Iraqi Airways

Invicta International Airlines

Head office: Manston Airport, Ramsgate, Kent, England.
Founded: 1970, succeeding Invicta Air Cargo, a purely cargo-carrying concern. In 1974 Invicta was merged into the European Ferries group.
Routes: Passenger and cargo charter flights and inclusive-tour operations, principally flown from Manston and Luton.
Aircraft operated: Boeing 720 and Vanguard.

Above left The flying horse insignia of charter operator Invicta Airlines.
Centre left and top right The symbol of Iraqi Airways displayed on a Boeing 737.
Below and bottom right The ancient mythical symbol of Persia, the Homa Bird, carried on the tail of a 737 (below) and 727 (right) of Iran Air.

Iran Air (Iran National Airlines Corporation)

Head office: Iran Air Building, Mehrabad Airport, Teheran, Iran.
Founded: 1962, following the government merger of two private airline companies.
Routes: Domestic services to 18 points. Regional and international services to London, Frankfurt, Paris, Athens, Geneva, Rome, Moscow, Istanbul, Kuwait, Doha, Dubai, Abu Dhabi, Bahrain and Dhahran, and to India, Pakistan and Afghanistan. Charter operations are also undertaken.
Aircraft operated: Boeing 707, 727, 737, 747; Douglas DC-6; Concorde on option.

Iraqi Airways

Head office: New International Airport, Baghdad, Iraq.
Founded: 1945, initially as a subsidiary of Iraqi State Railways, becoming fully independent in 1960.
Routes: Scheduled services from Baghdad to Basra, Mosul, London, Paris, Berlin, Frankfurt, Geneva, Prague, Vienna, Athens, Istanbul, Beirut, Damascus, Amman, Cairo, Teheran, Kuwait, Bahrain, Dhahran, Doha, Karachi, New Delhi, with seasonal services to Jeddah.
Aircraft operated: Trident One; Viscount; Antonov An-12, An-24; Boeing 707, 737.

Above A JAT Boeing 727, used by the Yugoslavian airline on its European routes. JAT (symbol opposite) is unusual among Eastern European airlines in having purchased jets from America.

Below A Japan Airlines 747, usually to be seen on JAL's North American services and on the Polar route from Tokyo to Europe via Anchorage. The latter route extends via both Moscow and Karachi/Delhi/Bangkok back to Tokyo but normally utilizes more than one plane and cannot strictly be called a round-the-world service.

Overleaf A Japan Airlines Boeing 747 taxi-ing at Tokyo's Haneda International Airport.

Japan Air Lines (Jal-Nihon Koku Kabushiki Kaisha)

Head office: Tokyo Building, 2-chome, Marunouchi, Chiyoda-ku, Tokyo, Japan.
Founded: 1953, taking over the original privately-owned airline of the same name (founded 1951).
Routes: Domestic services in operation to major cities in Japan, and Okinawa. Extensive network of international services to points in Asia, Australia, North and Central America, the Middle East and Europe.
Aircraft operated: Boeing 747, 727; Douglas DC-10, DC-8; Beech 18.

Jugoslovenski Aerotransport (JAT)

Head office: PO Box 749, Bircaninova 1-111, Belgrade, Jugoslavia.
Founded: 1946.
Routes: Domestic network links principal cities. International services from Belgrade and Zagreb to Athens, Beirut, Cairo, Copenhagen, Frankfurt, Munich, Paris, London, Vienna, Rome, Milan, Venice, Sofia, Budapest, Prague, Moscow, Warsaw, Zurich, Amsterdam, East Berlin, Tunis, Tripoli, Stockholm and Istanbul.
Aircraft operated: Boeing 707, 727; Douglas DC-9; Caravelle.

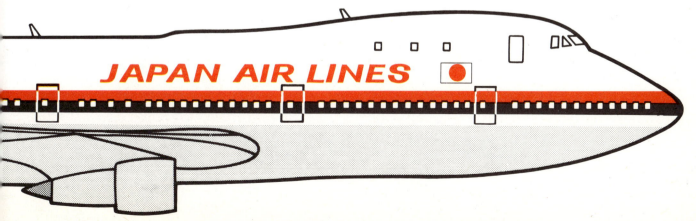

KLM-Royal Dutch Airlines

Head office: Amstelveen, Netherlands.
Founded: 1919, and is the world's oldest continuously operating airline.
Routes: International services from Amsterdam and Rotterdam to points in Europe, North and Latin America, the Near, Middle and Far East, Africa and Australia. There are four subsidiaries: KLM Aerocargo, KLM Noordzee Helicopters, NLM and KLM AIR CHARTER (founded 1971) which operates charter and inclusive-tour services.
Aircraft operated: Boeing 747; Douglas DC-10, DC-9, DC-8.

Korean Air Lines (KAL)

Head office: KAL Building, 118 2-ka, Namdaemun-ro, Chung-ku, Seoul, South Korea.
Founded: 1962, as successor to Korean National Airlines.
Routes: Domestic network linking Seoul to principal towns. International services to Tokyo, Osaka, Fukuoka, Taipei, Hong Kong, Bangkok, Honolulu and Los Angeles. Also a cargo service to Paris.
Aircraft operated: Boeing 747, 707, 727; Douglas DC-8; YS-11A; Fokker F.27.

Kuwait Airways

Head office: PO Box 394, Kuwait.
Founded: 1953, as Kuwait National Airways. Name changed to Kuwait Airways in 1958.
Routes: Services to most Middle East capital cities, to Bombay, Delhi, Muscat, Karachi and Aden, and to London via Frankfurt, Rome, Athens, Geneva and Paris.
Aircraft operated: Boeing 707.

Far left The tail of a KAL Boeing 727. *Centre* The insignia of Kuwait Airways. *Bottom* A DC-10 of KLM (Koninklijke Luchtvaart Maatschappij), used mainly on that airline's Far Eastern and North American services. KLM is the world's oldest airline and has very close ties with the Dutch charter operator Martinair. Both operate almost exclusively Douglas fleets but Martinair does have a single Fokker F.28. 'Prinses Margriet', which provides transport for the Dutch Royal family.

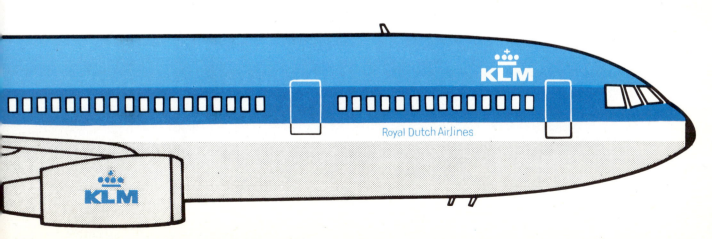

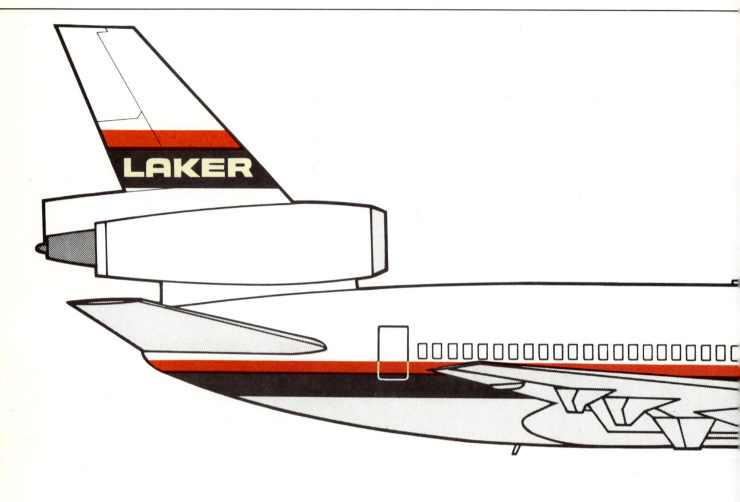

Above Passengers disembarking at Gatwick from a 707 in the colours of International Caribbean, a Laker Airways subsidiary flying between London and Seawell, Barbados.

Laker Airways

Head office: Gatwick Airport, Horley, Surrey, England.
Founded: 1966.
Routes: Contract inclusive-tour and charter operations. Also, provides the aircraft used by International Caribbean Airways, an associate company operating low-fare flights between London, Luxembourg and Barbados.
Aircraft operated: Douglas DC-10; Boeing 707; BAC 1-11.

Below A DC-10 of the British non-scheduled operator, Laker Airways. Laker initially acquired three of these aircraft, mainly for charters across the North Atlantic. Two were intended for use on problematic Skytrain 'walk-on' service from Stansted to New York and had the word 'Skytrain' printed prominently on one side. With the massive overcapacity on the North Atlantic route in 1974 and 1975, however, Laker ran into intense opposition from many interested parties.
Bottom One of the two Boeing 707s acquired by Laker second-hand from Qantas.

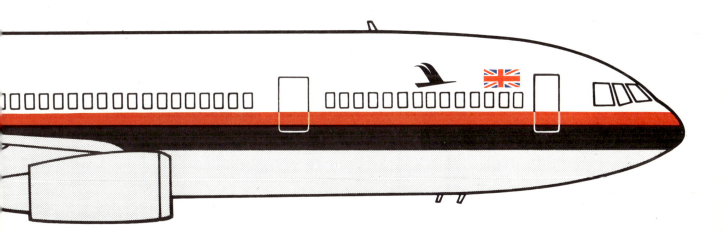

Lot-Polskie Linie Lotnicze

Head office: ul Grojecka 17, Warsaw, Poland.
Founded: 1929, in a government merger of two private airlines.
Routes: Domestic services between Warsaw and major cities in Poland. International services to Europe, the USA, Egypt, Iraq, Lebanon and Syria.
Aircraft operated: Ilyushin Il-62, Il-18; Tupolev Tu-134; Antonov An-24B.

Lufthansa (Deutsche Lufthansa AG)

Head office: 2-6 von Gablenz Strasse, D-5000 Cologne 21, West Germany.

Founded: 1926.

Routes: Domestic services link principal West German cities. Extensive network of world-wide services to major centres in Europe, North and South America, Africa, the Near, Middle and Far East, and Australia.

Aircraft operated: Boeing, 747, 707, 727, 737; Douglas DC-10; Airbus A300.

Luxair (Societe Anonyme Luxembourgeoise de Navigation Aerienne)

Head office: PO Box 2203, Luxembourg Airport, Luxembourg.

Founded: 1961, principally to act as a local service, carrying commuting businessmen to nearby foreign cities, and as a feeder line, transporting intercontinental passengers to major European gateways, and distributing cut-rate or charter passengers of non-IATA (International Air Transport Association) airlines to European centres. Services from Luxembourg to Amsterdam, Brussels, Geneva, London, Frankfurt, Paris and Rome, and to the holiday resorts of Athens, Gerona, Ibiza, Malaga, Nice, Palma, Rimini and Tunis (Cathage and Monastir). Also low-fare flights are operated to Johannesburg in conjunction with Luxavia SA.

Aircraft operated: Boeing 707; Caravelle and Fokker F.27.

Opposite top The symbol of LOT, the Polish national airline.
Below Luxair, one of the few scheduled international carriers which is not an IATA member, carries this symbol on its tail fins.
Bottom A DC-10 of Lufthansa, the West German flag carrier. Lufthansa has a non-IATA subsidiary, Condor, which is the largest wholly non-scheduled carrier of passengers in the world.

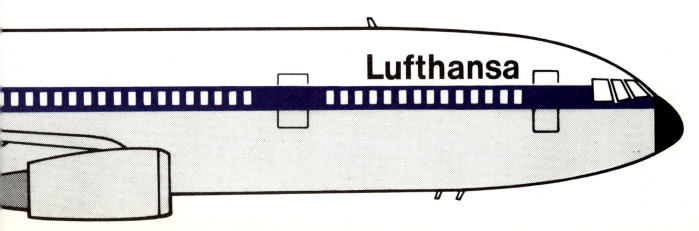

Malaysian Airline System (MAS)

Malaysian Airline System (MAS)

Head office: No 4 Jalan Sulieman, Kuala Lumpur, Malaysia.
Founded: 1971, succeeding the jointly operated Malaysia-Singapore Airlines.
Routes: Domestic services to principal cities and towns. International services to Singapore, Bangkok, Haadyai, Jakarta, Medan, Hong Kong, Bandar Seri, Bangawan, Taipei and trunk routes to London and Tokyo.
Aircraft operated: Boeing 707, 737; Fokker F.27; BN-2A Islander.

Malev (Magyar Legikoz-Lekedesi Vallalat)

Head office: V Vörösmarty-ter 5, Budapest, Hungary.
Founded: 1946, as Maszovlet. Name changed to Malev in 1954.
Routes: International services to major towns in Europe, including Scandinavia, USSR, the Middle East and North Africa.
Aircraft operated: Tupolev Tu-154, Tu-134, Ilyushin Il-18.

Middle East Airlines Airliban

Head office: PO Box 206, Beirut International Airport, Lebanon
Founded: 1945, as Middle East Airlines. Name changed to Middle East Airlines Airliban in 1965 following a merger with Air Liban. In 1969, Lebanese International Airways was also taken over.
Routes: Network of services radiating from Beirut to points in the Middle East, Asia, Europe and Africa.
Aircraft operated: Boeing 747, 707, 720; Caravelle.

Monarch Airlines

Head office: Luton Airport, Luton, Beds, England.
Founded: 1967.
Routes: Inclusive-tour and world-wide charter services operated.
Aircraft operated: Boeing 720.

Left The tail of a Boeing 737 of MAS, the Malaysian national airline.
Opposite top The symbol of the Hungarian airline Malev and (below) the same displayed in reverse on a Tu-134.
Opposite bottom left The Cedars of Lebanon, symbol of Middle East Airlines which is based in Beirut.
Opposite bottom right The unmistakable insignia of British charter operator, Monarch Airlines. Monarch was the last airline in Europe to keep the Bristol Britannia in passenger operation.

Malev (Magyar Legikoz–Lekedesi Vallalat)
Middle East Airlines Airliban
Monarch Airlines

121

MOUNT COOK AIRLINES

Mount Cook Airlines

Head office: Private Bag, Christchurch, New Zealand.

Founded: The company has its origins in the New Zealand Aero Transport Company, founded in 1920 for charter operations. Scheduled services were begun in 1961.

Routes: Domestic services link Christchurch with Mount Cook, Queenstown, Milford Sound, Te Anau, Rotorua and Auckland; Dunedin with Alexandra and Queenstown; and Auckland with Waiheke Island, Pakotoa Island, Kawan Islands and Waitangi. Tourist and charter services are also undertaken.

Aircraft operated: HS748; Douglas DC-3; BN-2A Islander; Grumman Super Goose, Widgeon; Fletcher FU-24; Cessna 180, 185.

National Airlines

Head office: PO Box 2055, AMF, Miami, Florida 33159, USA.

Founded: 1934.

Routes: Services from Miami along the Atlantic coast up to New York and Boston and along the Gulf of Mexico and across to the Pacific coast to New Orleans, Houston, San Diego, Los Angeles and San Francisco. Also a daily service to London is operated.

Aircraft operated: Boeing 747, 727; Douglas DC-10, DC-8.

Opposite page top The Mount Cook Lily, symbol of the internal New Zealand airline.
Left One of the three Hawker Siddeley 748s operated by Mount Cook Airlines.
Above The 'Sunshine' insignia of National Airlines on the tail of a Douglas DC-10. National use this aircraft on their only international route—Miami to London Heathrow—as well as for their 'bread and butter' services from the northeast states to Florida.

New Zealand National Airways Corporation (NZNAC)
Nigeria Airways

New Zealand National Airways Corporation (NZNAC)

Head office: PO Box 96, Wellington C1, New Zealand.
Founded: 1945, to take over and expand existing domestic airline services.
Routes: Inter- and intra-island operations, with services to 25 points on New Zealand's North and South Islands.
Aircraft operated: Boeing 737; Viscount; Fokker F.27.

Nigeria Airways

Head office: PO Box 136, Airways House, Lagos Airport, Nigeria.
Founded: 1958, as WAAC (Nigeria) to take over the operations of the West African Airways Corporation. Name changed to Nigeria Airways in 1971.
Routes: Domestic services from Lagos and Kano to principal towns in Nigeria. International services to London, Rome, Zurich, Madrid, Accra, Abidjan, Monrovia, Freetown, Bathurst, Dakar, Beirut and New York.
Aircraft operated: Boeing 707, 737; Fokker F.28, F.27; Aztec.

Left The tail of a Boeing 737 of New Zealand's internal airline, National Airways Corporation.
Above A Nigeria Airways Fokker F.27.
Right The delightful insignia of the Nigerian airline.

124

Northwest Airlines
Olympic Airways

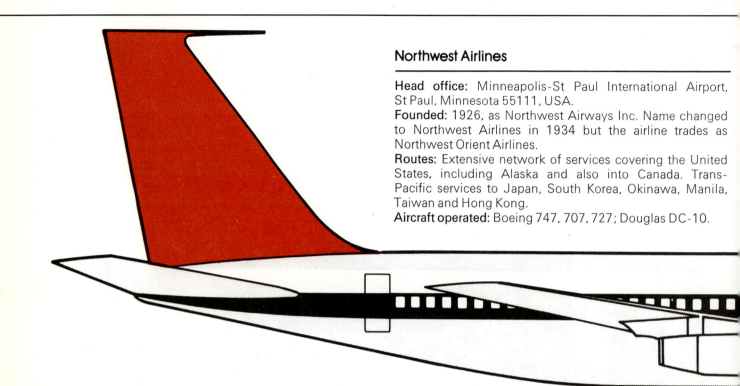

Northwest Airlines

Head office: Minneapolis-St Paul International Airport, St Paul, Minnesota 55111, USA.

Founded: 1926, as Northwest Airways Inc. Name changed to Northwest Airlines in 1934 but the airline trades as Northwest Orient Airlines.

Routes: Extensive network of services covering the United States, including Alaska and also into Canada. Trans-Pacific services to Japan, South Korea, Okinawa, Manila, Taiwan and Hong Kong.

Aircraft operated: Boeing 747, 707, 727; Douglas DC-10.

Olympic Airways

Head office: 96 Syngrou Avenue, Athens, Greece.

Founded: 1957.

Routes: Domestic services between the principal Greek cities and islands. International services to Australia, Cyprus, Egypt, France, Germany, Israel, Italy, Lebanon, Netherlands, Switzerland, Turkey, UK and the USA.

Aircraft operated: Boeing 747, 707, 720, 727; YS-11A.

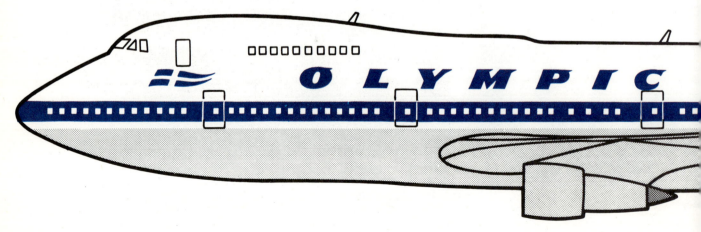

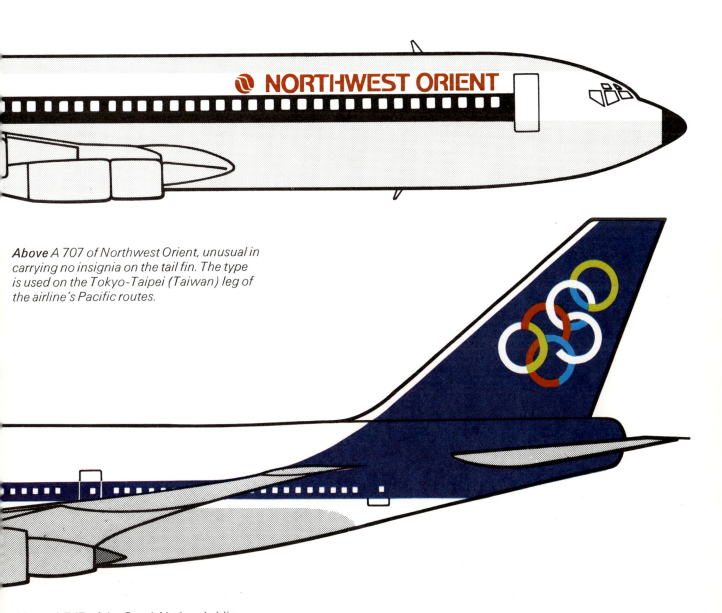

Above A 707 of Northwest Orient, unusual in carrying no insignia on the tail fin. The type is used on the Tokyo-Taipei (Taiwan) leg of the airline's Pacific routes.

Above A 747 of the Greek National airline, easily identified by the familiar Olympic rings on the tail. Until the end of 1974 the airline was operated by Aristotle Onassis on behalf of the Greek government. The blue and white motif below the cockpit is from the Greek national flag.

Pakistan International Airlines Corporation (PIA)

Head office: PIA Building, Karachi Airport, Pakistan.
Founded: 1955, in a Government take-over of Orient Airways.
Routes: Domestic services to major cities and towns within Pakistan. International services to Europe, USSR, the Middle and Far East, including Peking, and to New York.
Aircraft operated: Douglas DC-10; Boeing 707, 720B; Fokker F.27.

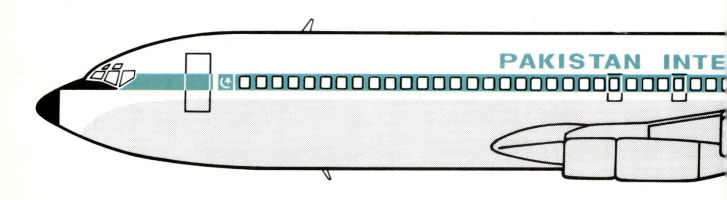

Overseas National Airways (ONA)

Head office: Kennedy International Airport, Jamaica, New York 11430, USA.
Founded: 1950.
Routes: Charter operations undertaken on a domestic basis and to the Caribbean, Europe, and east to India.
Aircraft operated: Douglas DC-10, DC-9, DC-8; Electra freighter.

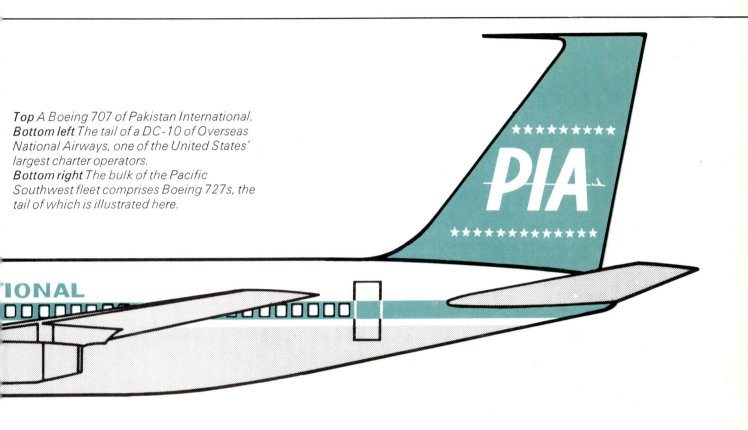

Top A Boeing 707 of Pakistan International.
Bottom left The tail of a DC-10 of Overseas
National Airways, one of the United States'
largest charter operators.
Bottom right The bulk of the Pacific
Southwest fleet comprises Boeing 727s, the
tail of which is illustrated here.

Pacific Southwest Airlines (PSA)

Head office: 3226 North Harbor Drive, San
Diego, California 92101, USA.
Founded: 1945, to operate solely within the
state of California.
Routes: Intra-state services to San Diego,
Long Beach, Los Angeles, San Jose, San
Francisco, Sacramento, Hollywood/Burbank,
Ontario, Fresno, Stockton, Oakland.
Aircraft operated: Boeing 727; TriStar.

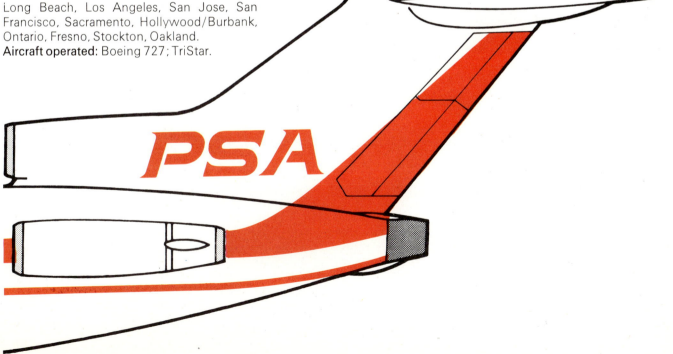

Pan American World Airways

Head office: Pan Am Building, New York, 10017, USA.
Founded: 1927, and has since developed into one of the world's leading airlines. Pan Am derives more income from intercontinental air traffic than any other carrier in the world. Apart from scheduled operations and involvement in various foreign airlines, Pan American's numerous interests include the Intercontinental chain of hotels, the operation of a general aviation airport and a heliport in the New York area, the American distribution of the Dassault Fan Jet

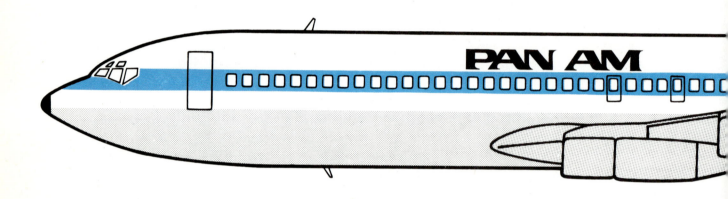

Falcon, and the responsibility of being the prime contractor to the Defense Department in the operation of the Cape Canaveral Missile Test Centre and the down-range missile tracking station.

Routes: World-wide network of routes to major cities in every continent. A network of local services is also operated in Germany. Pan Am are the only scheduled American airline *not* allowed to work domestic services in the USA. Pan Am operate a daily 'round-the-world' service (PA1 and PA2) in both directions.

Aircraft operated: Boeing 747, 707, 727.

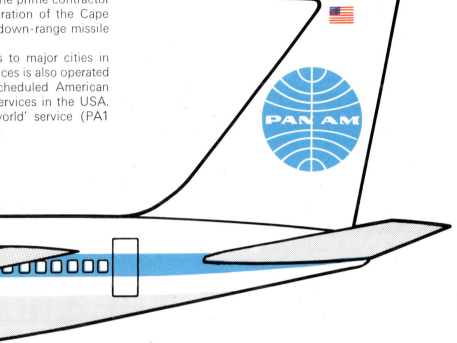

Philippine Airlines (PAL)

Head office: PAL Building, Ayala Avenue, Makati, Rizal, Philippines.

Founded: 1945. PAL took over Air Manila and Filipinas Orient Airways in 1974.

Routes: Air transport is an essential element in domestic and international commerce for the Philippine Islands group. Domestic services link Manila and major towns and cities within the islands. International services are operated to the USA, Australia, Japan, Hong Kong, Taiwan, Singapore, Thailand, Pakistan, Italy, the Netherlands and West Germany.

Aircraft operated: Douglas DC-10, DC-8, DC-3; BAC 1-11; HS748.

Previous pages The flagship of the Pan American fleet *'Jet Clipper America'*, registered appropriately as N747PA and later leased to Air Zaire. The lettering of Pan Am has recently been changed and the new style can be seen *(above)* on this 707. Pan Am was the first airline to operate both the 747 and the 707, though with the former taking over the most important routes, the 707s are now normally employed on the less dense routes, such as those in the Pacific, or, increasingly, for cargo.

Far left A Philippine Airlines DC-10, used mainly on the important Hong Kong – Manila – San Francisco trunk route. The tail insignia is used only on international flights.

Left The tail of a Philippines DC-8, showing the insignia used on internal flights in the islands.

Qantas Airways
Sabena-Belgian World Airlines (Societe Anonyme
Belge d'Exploitation de la Navigation Aerienne)

Qantas Airways

Head office: 70 Hunter Street, Sydney, New South Wales, Australia.

Founded: The company's origins lie in the Queensland and Northern Territory Aerial Services Limited founded in 1920. (The name 'Qantas' coming from the initial letters). Qantas Empire Airways was formed in 1934 by Qantas and Imperial Airways originally to operate the Brisbane-Singapore section of the England-Australia service. Name changed to Qantas Airways in 1967. Services incorporating Melbourne, Sydney, Brisbane and Perth within the international network of routes to London via Singapore and points in the Far, Middle and Near East, and Europe; to Vancouver via Fiji, Honolulu and San Francisco; to New Zealand, New Guinea, Manila, Hong Kong, Tokyo, Noumea, Norfolk Island and Johannesburg via Mauritius.

Aircraft operated: Boeing 747, 707; Douglas DC-4; HS125.

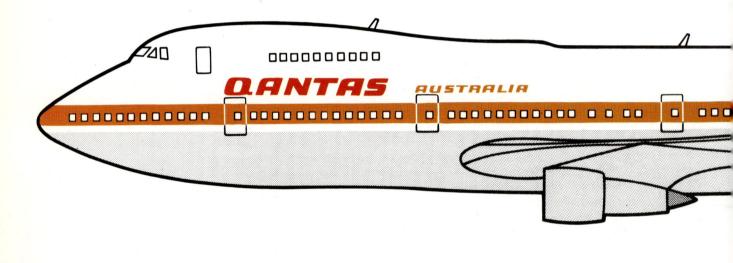

Sabena-Belgian World Airlines (Societe Anonyme Belge d'Exploitation de la Navigation Aerienne)

Head office: 35 Rue Cardinal Mercier, 1000 Brussels, Belgium.

Founded: 1923, to succeed the pioneer airline SNETA. Sobelair is a subsidiary of Sabena, operating charter and inclusive-tour flights.

Routes: International services to major European cities; to Bombay, Bangkok, Singapore, Manila and Tokyo in the Far East; to Montreal, New York, Guatemala City, Mexico City, Santiago and Buenos Aires in North, Central and South America; to the Middle East; and to points in Africa including Kinshasa (capital of the former Belgian colony of the Congo, now Zaire, where Sabena had previously concentrated much effort in developing a domestic network) and Johannesburg.

Aircraft operated: Boeing 747, 707, 727, 737; Douglas DC-10; Caravelle; Fokker F.27; Cessna 310; SIAI-Marchetti SF260.

Right The recently adopted Sabena symbol on the tail of a 707, an aircraft the Belgian airline uses on a variety of routes including, surprisingly, Brussels—London.
Opposite page A Sabena 747 on take-off; the 747s are used mainly for Brussels—New York traffic.

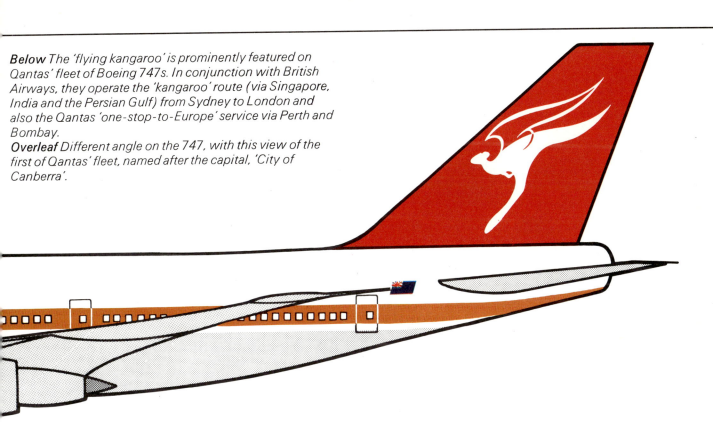

Below The 'flying kangaroo' is prominently featured on Qantas' fleet of Boeing 747s. In conjunction with British Airways, they operate the 'kangaroo' route (via Singapore, India and the Persian Gulf) from Sydney to London and also the Qantas 'one-stop-to-Europe' service via Perth and Bombay.
Overleaf Different angle on the 747, with this view of the first of Qantas' fleet, named after the capital, 'City of Canberra'.

Scandinavian Airlines System (SAS)

Scandinavian Airlines System (SAS)

Head office: Bromma Airport, 16187 Bromma, Sweden.

Founded: Originally in 1946, as a consortium of three existing Scandinavian airlines, and now the international airline of Sweden, Norway and Denmark. The activities of the companies were fully integrated in 1950. SAS has a minority interest in Thai Airways International and shares the operation of their Europe-Australia route.

Routes: SAS pioneered and established the first Polar routes to the American West Coast and the Far East. Current services are operated within Scandinavia and Europe, including USSR; to Africa, the Middle and Far East, and to North, Central and South America.

Aircraft operated: Boeing 747; Douglas DC-10, DC-9, DC-8; Convair CV-440.

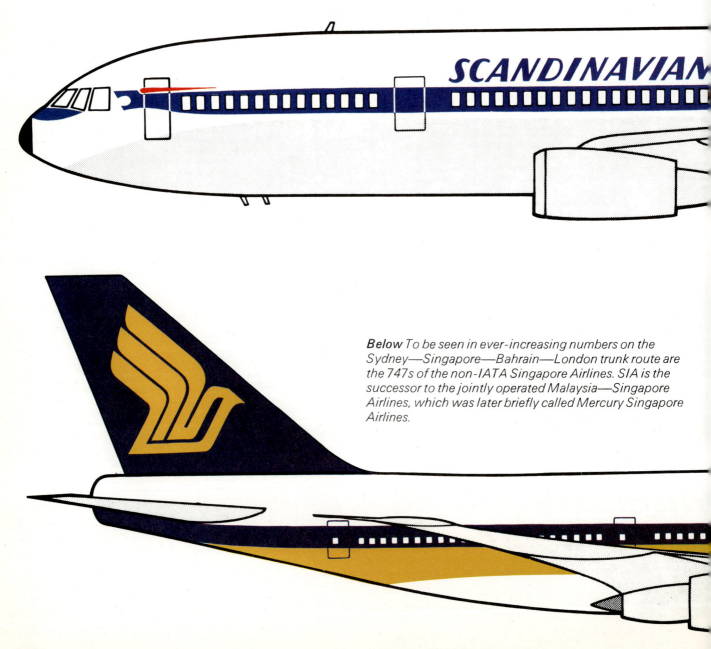

Below To be seen in ever-increasing numbers on the Sydney—Singapore—Bahrain—London trunk route are the 747s of the non-IATA Singapore Airlines. SIA is the successor to the jointly operated Malaysia—Singapore Airlines, which was later briefly called Mercury Singapore Airlines.

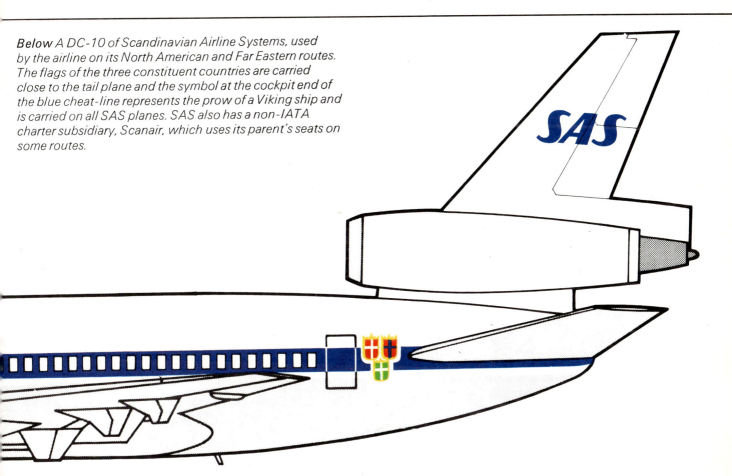

Below A DC-10 of Scandinavian Airline Systems, used by the airline on its North American and Far Eastern routes. The flags of the three constituent countries are carried close to the tail plane and the symbol at the cockpit end of the blue cheat-line represents the prow of a Viking ship and is carried on all SAS planes. SAS also has a non-IATA charter subsidiary, Scanair, which uses its parent's seats on some routes.

Singapore Airlines (SIA)

Head office: SIA Building, 77 Robinson Road, Singapore.
Founded: 1972, succeeding the jointly-operated Malaysia-Singapore Airlines.
Routes: Services from Singapore are operated to Kuala Lumpur, Saigon, Manila, Brunei, Madras, Medan; to London via Colombo, Bombay, Bahrain, Athens, Rome, Zurich, Amsterdam and Frankfurt; to Tokyo and Osaka via Bangkok, Hong Kong and Taipei; and to Sydney, Melbourne, and Perth via Djakarta.
Aircraft operated: Boeing 747, 707, 737.

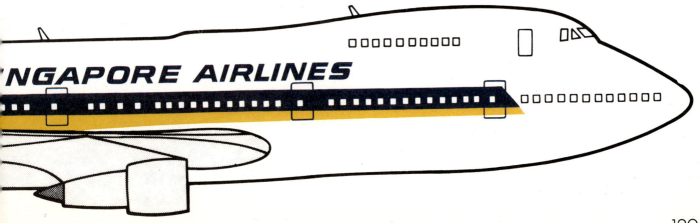

South African Airways (Suid-Afrikaanse Lugdiens)
Swissair (Schweizerische Luftverkehr)

South African Airways (Suid-Afrikaanse Lugdiens)

Head office: SA Airways Centre, Johannesburg, South Africa.
Founded: 1934.
Routes: Network of domestic routes within South Africa. Regional services to South West Africa, Rhodesia, Malawi, Mozambique, Botswana, Mauritius, Swaziland, Lesotho and Malagasy. International services to Sydney via Mauritius and Perth; Rio de Janeiro, and New York via Ilha do Sal; Buenos Aires; and to Lisbon, Madrid, Rome, Athens, Frankfurt, Zurich, Vienna, Paris, Luxembourg, Brussels, Amsterdam and London via Salisbury, Luanda, Las Palmas and Ilha do Sol.
Aircraft operated: Boeing 747, 707, 727, 737; HS748.

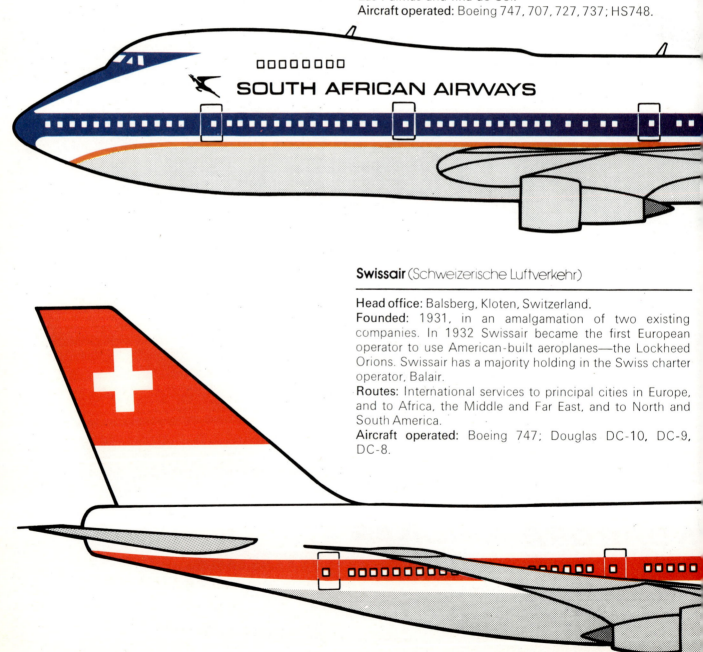

Swissair (Schweizerische Luftverkehr)

Head office: Balsberg, Kloten, Switzerland.
Founded: 1931, in an amalgamation of two existing companies. In 1932 Swissair became the first European operator to use American-built aeroplanes—the Lockheed Orions. Swissair has a majority holding in the Swiss charter operator, Balair.
Routes: International services to principal cities in Europe, and to Africa, the Middle and Far East, and to North and South America.
Aircraft operated: Boeing 747; Douglas DC-10, DC-9, DC-8.

Below *One of the South African Airways 747s which can operate non-stop between London Heathrow and Johannesburg, despite overflying sea almost the whole way to avoid the 'bulge' of Africa. With the independence in 1975 of the Portuguese colonies of the Cape Verde Islands and Angola, SAA were in danger of losing their refuelling stops (at Ilha do Sal and Luanda) and may, therefore, equip all their 747s to make this 12-hour journey non-stop. All SAA planes have the English language name on one side of the plane and the Afrikaans equivalent, Suid-Afrikaanse Lugdiens, on the other. The animal insignia is the Springbok.*

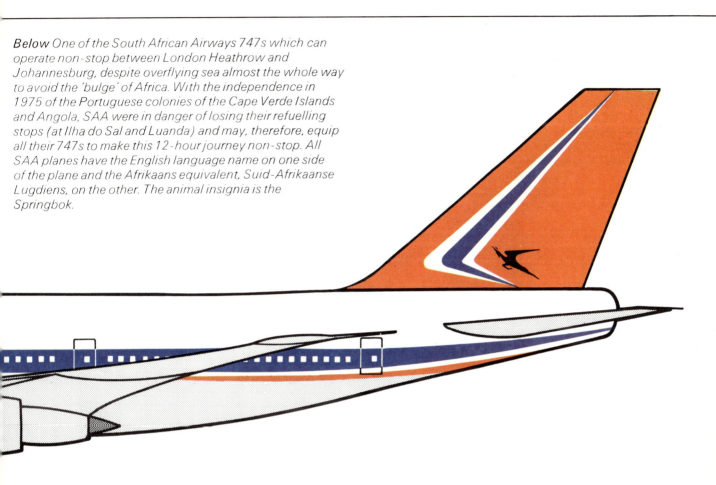

Below *One of the Swissair 747s used by that airline for its New York services. Swissair also has an associated non-IATA company, Balair, which uses the same livery.*

141

Thai Airways International
Trans-Australia Airlines (TAA)

Thai Airways International

Head office: 1043 Phaholyothin Road, Bangkok 4, Thailand.
Founded: 1959, by Thai Airways Corporation and SAS, the latter providing technical, administrative and operational assistance. Usually known as Thai International.
Routes: Services from Bangkok to Hong Kong, Denpasar, Calcutta, Dacca, Delhi, Jakarta, Kathmandu, Kuala Lumpur, Manila, Osaka, Penang, Rangoon, Saigon, Singapore, Taipei, Tokyo, Sydney, Copenhagen, London and Frankfurt.
Aircraft operated: Douglas DC-10, DC-8.

Trans-Australia Airlines (TAA)

Head office: 50-56 Franklin Street, Melbourne, Victoria, Australia.
Founded: 1946, as a nationalized alternative to the private companies.
Routes: As the largest airline in the southern hemisphere in terms of revenue and passengers, TAA has an extensive domestic network throughout the states of Australia, Other activities include the service and maintenance of aircraft for the Bureau of Mineral Resources, and for flying doctor services.
Aircraft operated: Boeing 727; Douglas DC-9, DC-3; Fokker F.27; Twin Otter.

Left The tail of a Thai International DC-8.
Above The majority of Thai's international services are operated by DC-8s, including the London—Bangkok—Sydney trunk route. The registration on the fuselage reveals that this aircraft is on loan from SAS.
Below A Douglas DC-9 of Trans-Australia Airlines, which shares the domestic traffic in Australia roughly equally with the Ansett group.

Transportes Aereos Portugueses (TAP)

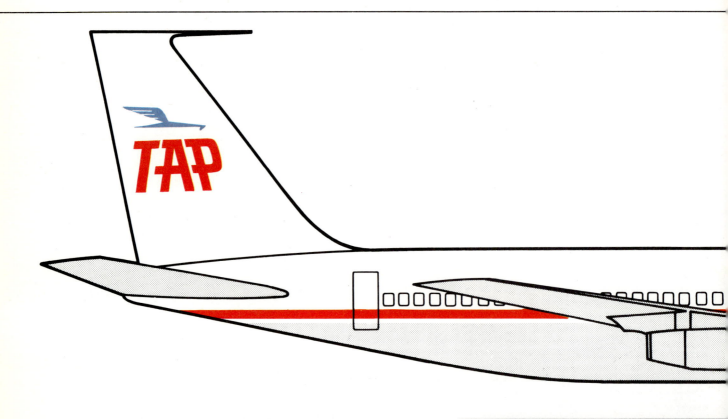

Transportes Aereos Portugueses (TAP)

Head office: Apartado 5194, Aeroporto de Lisboa, Lisbon, Portugal.
Founded: 1944.
Routes: Domestic services from Lisbon to Porto, Faro, Funchal, Porto Santo and Santa Maria. International services to Amsterdam, Brussels, Buenos Aires, Boston, Copenhagen, Dusseldorf, Frankfurt, Geneva, Johannesburg, Las Palmas, London, Madrid, Montreal, New York, Paris, Recife, Rio de Janeiro, Salisbury, Sao Paulo, Zurich and the formerly Portuguese territories Beira, Bissau, Lourenço Marques, and Luanda.
Aircraft operated: Boeing 747, 707, 727; Caravelle.

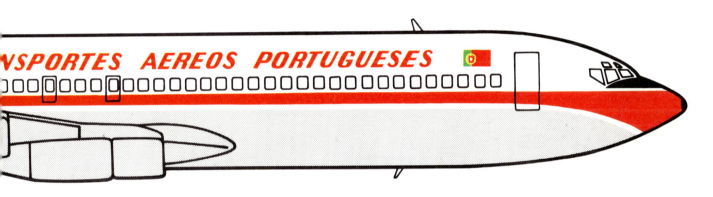

NSPORTES AEREOS PORTUGUESES

Above _A Boeing 707 of TAP, an airline operating nine of the type at the beginning of 1975._
Left _The flagship of the TAP fleet, Boeing 747 'Portugal'. With the sudden independence of Portugal's former colonies (Bissau, Angola, Mozambique, Cape Verde) in 1974 and 1975 there were doubts about the fleet's exact future requirements should there be restrictions on services to the newly independent states. Traffic from Lisbon to the African dependencies provided much of TAP's long-distance traffic before 1975, particularly with their 747s._

Below The colours carried by TWA up to and including 1975, displayed on a Boeing 707. TWA use this aircraft on both internal and trans-continental routes where the traffic density does not warrant a 747.
Above In 1975 an experimental design was being tried out on a 747, photographed here at London Heathrow. It retains the familiar red and white of TWA and, if adopted, will be the first change of livery by the airline for over 15 years.
Opposite page The insignia of Turkey's THY.

Trans World Airlines (TWA)

Head office: 605 Third Avenue, New York, NY 10016, USA.
Founded: A series of mergers involving several airline companies founded in the 1920s resulted in the formation of Transcontinental and Western Air (TWA) in 1930. Name changed to Trans World Airlines in 1950. Discussions early in 1975 suggest that a merger with the USA's other flag carrier, Pan Am, is likely in the future.
Routes: As the world's seventh largest airline in terms of passengers carried and the second flag carrier of the USA, TWA operates a transcontinental and inter-state network within the USA, and a round-the-world service to points in Europe, Africa and the Middle and Far East.
Aircraft operated: Boeing 747, 707, 727; TriStar; Douglas DC-9.

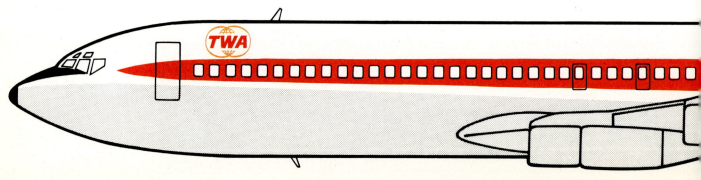

Turk Hava Yollari (THY)

Head office: Cumhuriyet Caddesi 199-201, Harbiye-Istanbul, Turkey.
Founded: 1933, as Devlet Hava Yollari (DHY). Name change to Turk Hava Yollari in 1956.
Routes: Domestic services linking principal Turkish cities. International services from Istanbul and Ankara to Vienna, Athens, Rome, Paris, Zurich, Munich, Milan, Geneva, Copenhagen, Frankfurt, Amsterdam, London, Brussels, Nicosia, Tel-Aviv and Beirut.
Aircraft operated: Boeing 707, 727; Douglas DC-10, DC-9; Fokker F.28.

Union de Transports Aeriens (UTA)
United Airlines (UAL)

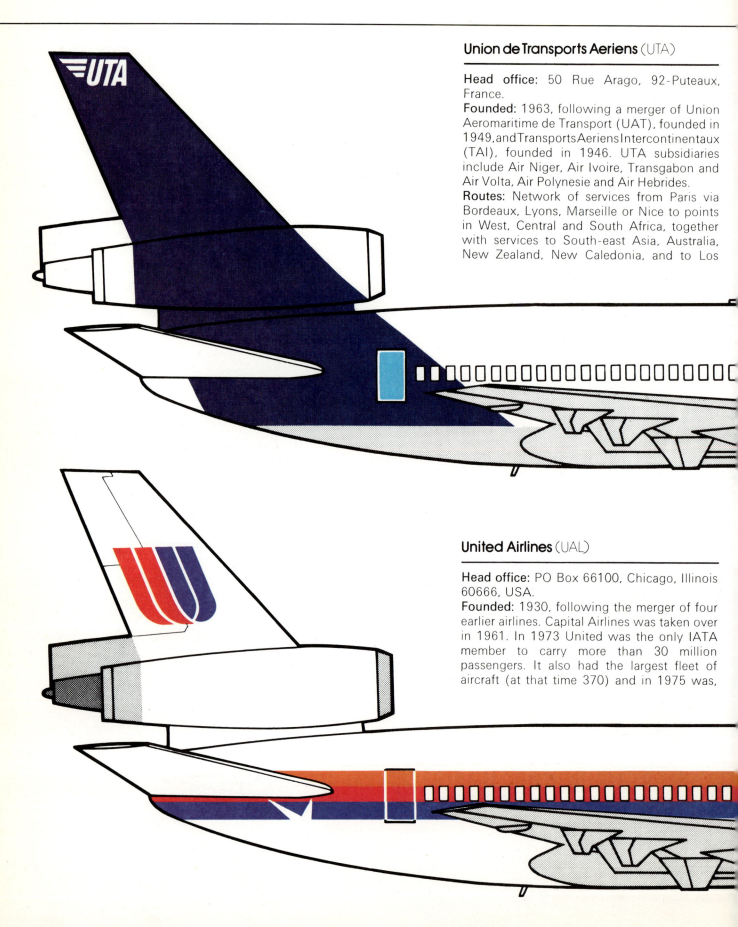

Union de Transports Aeriens (UTA)

Head office: 50 Rue Arago, 92-Puteaux, France.

Founded: 1963, following a merger of Union Aeromaritime de Transport (UAT), founded in 1949, and Transports Aeriens Intercontinentaux (TAI), founded in 1946. UTA subsidiaries include Air Niger, Air Ivoire, Transgabon and Air Volta, Air Polynesie and Air Hebrides.

Routes: Network of services from Paris via Bordeaux, Lyons, Marseille or Nice to points in West, Central and South Africa, together with services to South-east Asia, Australia, New Zealand, New Caledonia, and to Los

United Airlines (UAL)

Head office: PO Box 66100, Chicago, Illinois 60666, USA.

Founded: 1930, following the merger of four earlier airlines. Capital Airlines was taken over in 1961. In 1973 United was the only IATA member to carry more than 30 million passengers. It also had the largest fleet of aircraft (at that time 370) and in 1975 was,

Angeles via Polynesia and Honolulu. Local services are also operated within the New Hebrides and inclusive-tour flights under-taken.

Aircraft operated: Douglas DC-10, DC-8.

Below A DC-10 of UTA, France's second airline and Europe's largest independent operator. The airline uses the DC-10 on its African and Australasian routes, the latter being part of a lengthy 'round-the-world' service via Los Angeles, Tahiti, Fiji, Singapore and Karachi, operated in conjunction with Air France.

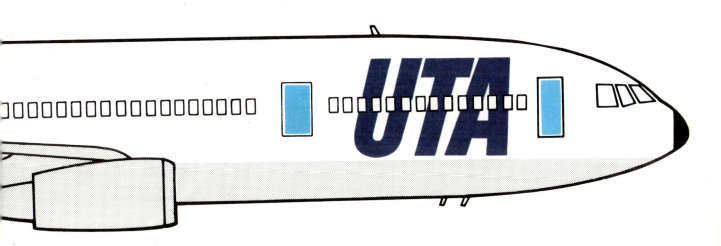

with the possible exception of Aeroflot, the largest airline in the world.

Routes: Extensive network of services within the USA, linking cities along the Atlantic seaboard and providing trans-continental services to cities on the Pacific coastline with links from Mexico to Vancouver in Canada, and to Hawaii.

Aircraft operated: Boeing 747, 727, 737; Douglas DC-10, DC-8.

Below The largest airline in the United States. United changed its colour scheme in 1974, and the new scheme is illustrated on this DC-10, an aircraft used for many of the airline's medium distance routes, such as Chicago—New York.

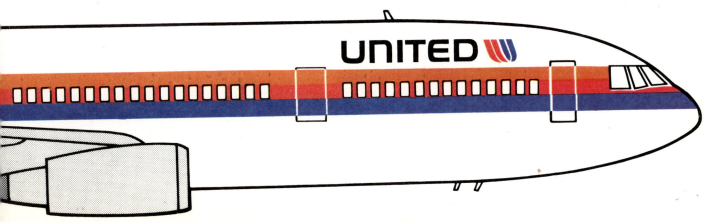

Varig (Empresa de Viacao Aerea Rio Grandense)

Head office: Edificio Varig, Aeroporto Santos Dumont, Rio de Janeiro, Brazil.
Founded: 1927.
Routes: Extensive network of services throughout Central and South America. International services to the USA, Europe, Africa and Asia. A round-the-world service is also projected.
Aircraft operated: Boeing 707, 727, 737; Electra; HS748; Douglas DC-10.

Below A DC-10 of Varig, the Brazilian overseas carrier, used principally on the airline's New York and European routes from Rio de Janeiro. Note the spelling of Brasil and the Brazilian flag.

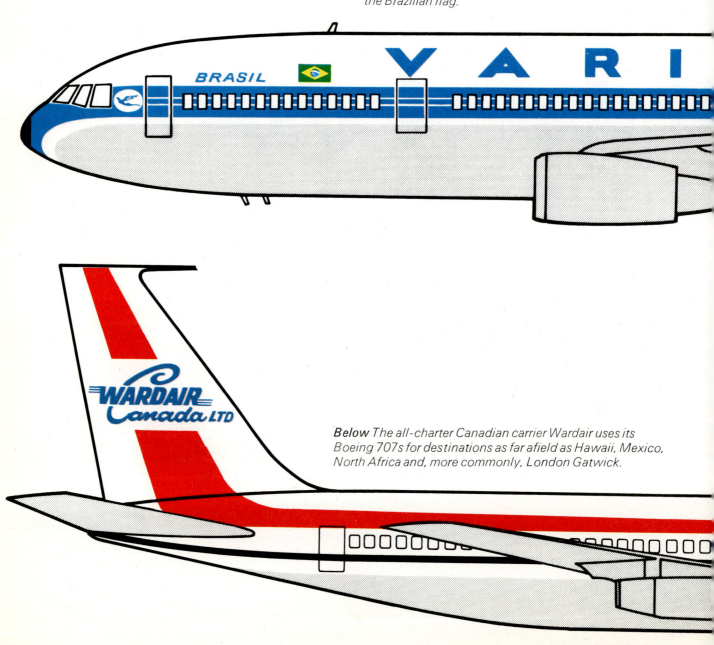

Below The all-charter Canadian carrier Wardair uses its Boeing 707s for destinations as far afield as Hawaii, Mexico, North Africa and, more commonly, London Gatwick.

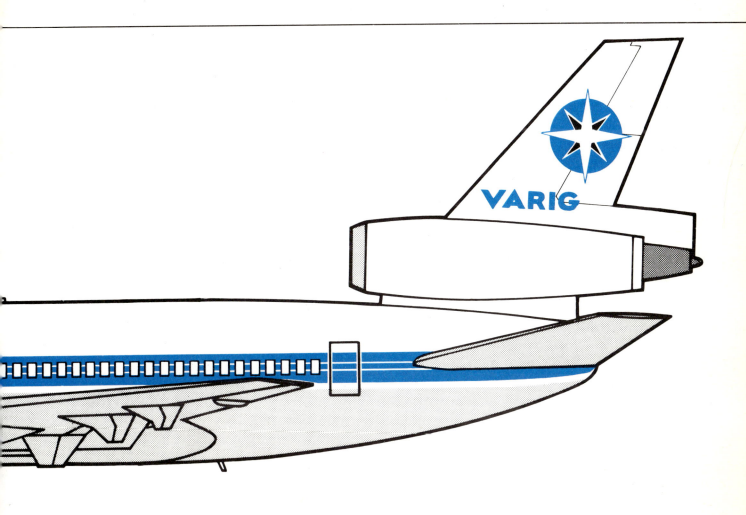

Wardair Canada

Head office: 26th Floor, C. N. Tower, Edmonton, Alberta, Canada.

Founded: Original company formed in 1946 as the Polaris Charter Company to serve the growing mining industry of the North-West Territories. Wardair was formed in 1952 to continue these operations. Name changed to Wardair Canada in 1962.

Routes: Domestic and international charter services.

Aircraft operated: Boeing 747, 707; Bristol Freighter; Twin Otter.

Western Airlines (WAL)
World Airways
Zambia Airways

Western Airlines (WAL)

Head office: 6060 Avion Drive, Los Angeles, California 90009, USA.
Founded: 1925, as Western Air Express, a pioneer in American airline operations. Name changed to Western Airlines in 1941.
Routes: Network of scheduled operations serving 12 western states, Alaska and Hawaii in the USA, Canada and Mexico.
Aircraft operated: Boeing 707, 720, 727, 737; Douglas DC-10.

World Airways

Head office: Oakland International Airport, Oakland, California 94614, USA.
Founded: 1948, as a non-scheduled airline.
Routes: World-wide passenger and cargo charter services from Oakland, California.
Aircraft operated: Boeing 747, 707, 727; Douglas DC-8.

Zambia Airways

Head office: PO Box 272, Lusaka City Airport, Zambia.
Founded: 1967.
Routes: Passenger services radiating from Lusaka to Zambia's eight provinces. International services to London, Rome, Nicosia, Nairobi, Dar-es-Salaam, Blantyre, Mauritius and Botswana, in association with Alitalia.
Aircraft operated: Douglas DC-8, BAC 1-11; HS748.

Below The insignia of World Airways, the largest of the United States wholly non-scheduled carriers.
Bottom right The tail of a DC-10 of California's Western Airlines.
Bottom left The motif of Zambia Airways, which dubs itself 'Eagle of Africa'.

ENGINE DETAILS
E1 fan
E2 stators
E3 air inlet doors
E4 by-pass
E5 manifolding
E6 cooler
E7 thrust reversers
E8 thrust cone

1 glass fibre radar cone
2 flight engineer's seat
3 flt eng electronics panel
4 staircase to. . .
5 upper first class lounge
6 forward passenger door
7 body frames
8 main frames
9 body bulkhead
10 engine start air (from APU)
11 load bearing floor
12 rear spar
13 undercarriage beam
14 retraction jacks
15 breaker strut actuator
16 main strut
17 brake reaction link
18 low profile tyres
19 undercarriage door
20 hot air manifold
21 keel box
22 centre keel
23 centre section fairing
24 centre passenger door
25 air conditioning ducts
26 galley
27 floor spars
28 freight floor